Guiding Light

By God Through Me
CYCLE B

Homilies by Fr. Joe Robinson

Shepherds of Christ Publications
P.O. Box 627
China, Indiana 47250 USA

Toll free USA: (888) 211-3041
Tel: (812) 273-8405
Fax: (812) 273-3182
Email: info@sofc.org
http://www.sofc.org

First Printing: 2014

Dedicated to Pope Francis

In Honor
of Our
Beloved Priests

The Mass

The Mass is the sacrifice of Calvary –
sacramentally made present.
As members of the mystical body
of Christ, we are united to all
the Masses going on around the
world this day. Our lives are an
offering to the Father, in union
with Jesus in the Holy Sacrifice
of the Mass, in the Holy Spirit,
through the intercession of
our Heavenly Mother –
with all the angels and saints
and the souls in purgatory.
We are one united to the Mass.
Tremendous grace can be
outpoured on the earth from
doing this, living in the Father's
will in love – united to the
Mass, the sacrifice of Calvary –
sacramentally made present.
God enlists our help today –

Oh the gift of the Mass –
Oh the gift of the priest –

Jesus is truly present in His Divinity
and humanity in the Eucharist –

He says:
"This is My Body,
   This is My Blood,
   given up for you."

Rita Robinson Ring, Co-founder
Shepherds of Christ Ministries

We want Adoration Chapels
around the world –
The Mighty Medicine

Table of Contents
Cycle B – 2014 / 2015

Dedicated to William and Alice Robinson.

Our Mother and Father married on
June 25, 1936 in St. Boniface Church, Cincinnati.

1st Sunday of Advent
November 27, 2011

INTRODUCTION – (Isaiah 63:16b-17. 19b; 64:2-7) In all the events of our daily lives, a true prophet has the ability to see God more profoundly than anyone else can. In our first reading taken from Isaiah, the prophet recognized that when the Babylonians invaded and destroyed Israel, it was a disaster that God's people brought upon themselves for having ignored the direction God had tried to give them. When they returned home after 50 years of captivity, the job of rebuilding what they had lost was enormous. The prophet laments how God's people are now suffering and, in the name of God's wayward people, the prophet prays for their heavenly Father to forgive them and help them. It is an extremely beautiful prayer.

HOMILY – (Mark 13:33-37) Today begins a new Church Year – designated as Cycle B. I might point out that our gospel today was written by St. Mark. Most of our gospels in Church Year Cycle A came from St. Matthew. Now this year we'll hear mostly from St. Mark. For many people that may not seem significant, but each gospel has its own unique features. Mark is the oldest gospel, written most probably in Rome sometime between the years 64-67. Tradition describes Mark as the interpreter of Peter. That is, he wrote down whatever he remembered of Peter's proclamation of the good news (that's what gospel means) about Jesus Christ. Matthew and Luke, who wrote for their own faith communities, borrowed heavily from Mark and included additional materials of their own. Today's gospel passage comes from Jesus' final days in Jerusalem. Mark is encouraging his community of believers to be strong in the face of persecution and to resist the temptations of the pagan world they lived in. He tells them Jesus is going to come again. Evil will be destroyed and those who have remained faithful will be rewarded with eternal life. Thus, when Jesus comes he will expect his followers to be living according to his teachings. If we remain aware that he might return at any time, perhaps when we least expect him, then we will be watchful. It is a message Mark is giving us as we begin the season of Advent. All that Jesus had to say to the people of his day, all that Mark wrote for his faith community, is a message that holds just as true for us today for it is more than human words. It is God's inspired Word.

Once there was a man who had a store and in order to protect his store he bought a big watchdog. His watchdog loved to curl up right across the doorway of the store to keep watch over the store. Unlike many watchdogs who are alerted at the slightest noise, this dog often fell asleep and kept sleeping even as people stepped over him to enter the store. Outside the store was a big sign: "Beware of dog." Visitors to the town would often ask why they had to beware of that dog sleeping in the doorway. The owner said, "well, before I put up the sign, people kept tripping over him." (taken from *Preaching Resources*, Nov. 27, 2011, pg 3) Not a good example of being watchful. A better example would be families who had a loved one serving in Iraq or Afghanistan for many months and who are now waiting for their loved one to come home in the near future. You can imagine their excitement and anticipation. Or perhaps you can think of the excitement and anticipation of a child who is waiting for Santa Claus, not knowing exactly when he might arrive.

We will soon celebrate Jesus' coming to us as an infant, but that was only the beginning of God's coming to us. Jesus continues to come through prayer, through charity toward others, through sacraments and Scripture and at the time of our death. Finally, he will come in glory at the end of the world. Advent is more than just to prepare us to celebrate Jesus' birth, it is a time for renewed awareness of God in our lives now and a time to be sure we are ready to meet him when he comes to take us into his eternal kingdom.

There are dozens of things a person might do to prepare themselves better spiritually. I will leave you with one suggestion: read the gospel for each day of Advent and think about it for several minutes. Where will you find the gospel? Get out your Bible, and look it up using the references in the bulletin each week or the references on the insert in today's bulletin. Amen.

2nd Sunday of Advent
December 4, 2011

INTRODUCTION – (Isaiah 40: 1-5, 9-11; 2 Peter 3:8-14; Mark 1:1-8) For the history behind today's first reading, we have to go back almost 600 years before Christ (587 years to be precise). We cannot imagine the devastation the Jewish people suffered under the Babylonians. It would have been the annihilation of any other nation, but since the Jews were God's special people, they were not to be exterminated. Their cities, their homes, their farms and the great temple built by Solomon almost 400 years earlier were all destroyed. Most of the Jews that weren't killed were taken as captives and slaves to Babylon, almost a 1000–mile trip, on foot, through modern day Lebanon, Syria, and Iraq. They slowly realized, through the words of the prophets, how they had abandoned their God and how that set the stage for this great disaster. But God promised not to abandon them; he assured them, through the prophets, that he would restore them to their homes and their lands. Roughly fifty years later the kingdom of the Babylonians was conquered and destroyed by the Persians (people who lived in Iran). The king of Persia, Cyrus, immediately gave the Jews permission to return to their land. Today's reading from Isaiah begins a large 16–chapter section of Isaiah known as the "Book of Consolation." The prophet is instructed by God to bring this good news to God's people. The route by which the Lord would lead his people home is referred to as "the way of the Lord." Attention must be given to preparing the way. This is the important theme in today's liturgy. John the Baptist takes up this theme five centuries later when he calls the people of his own day to prepare for the Messiah. The liturgy uses today's Scriptures to call us to prepare not only for Christmas but also for the various ways in which Christ comes to us in our daily lives as well as for the day when Christ will call us into his eternal kingdom.

HOMILY – Almost everything in life that is of any great importance requires preparation beforehand: getting an education, getting married, getting a job, moving, having a family (although sometimes the family accidentally turns out to be bigger than a person had planned on). When the pope or heads of state go to visit a place, preparations are made, often far in advance.

When God was about to send his only Son to earth to teach us and guide us into God's kingdom of unending peace and joy, he sent someone to prepare for that coming. St. Mark, as he begins his gospel, gets right to that point by telling us about John the Baptist. Actually, through the words of the prophets, God prepared for his Son's coming long before starting with Moses (Acts

3:22) and King David (Acts 2:25). He prepared for his Son's coming by preserving Jesus' mother from all sin, even original sin, which is the feast we celebrate this Thursday in the feast of the Immaculate Conception.

John the Baptist told God's people, and he tells us through the gospel, that even though God made many preparations beforehand for the coming of Jesus, we must prepare also. John called people to repent of their sins and change their ways if they were not living as God wanted. His baptism was a symbol of their starting a new way of life. John himself, although a holy man, adopted the lifestyle of the great prophet Elijah and his garments reflected his call to do penance. Many people thought maybe he was the Messiah, but John knew his role; he was only a voice calling people to prepare for One so much greater than he was that he was not worthy even to kneel down before him and untie his shoes.

We get very busy this time of the year preparing for Christmas and that's all very nice, but for many of us perhaps what we need to do to prepare is to become less busy and take time to reflect on what Christ's birth is all about. Last week I recommended that a very good way to prepare would be to read the gospel for the day, picture it, think about it for several minutes. Sometimes we can experience the Lord speaking to us in a powerful way through his Word. Or we could say the rosary during the week, or come to morning Mass or Holy Hour, or do some spiritual reading. There are hundreds of things we can do for other people too, but sometimes we need to take time to do something for ourselves in such a way that we are fed spiritually. As I said, perhaps we need to do less rather than more so we can use our time more efficiently. There's no substitute for quiet time. Taking quiet time for ourselves helps us to remain peaceful during such a busy time and helps us to keep our priorities in order. Don't just prepare for Christmas, prepare for Christ. Amen.

Feast of the Immaculate Conception
December 8, 2011

HOMILY – (Genesis 3:9-15, 20; Ephesians 1:3-6, 11-12; Luke 1:26-38) Today's feast of the Immaculate Conception begins with a story about our first parents. They had been blessed with every blessing God could give them. That is what the Garden of Eden represents. However, our first parents were not satisfied with what God gave them. They wanted to be as powerful as God who gave them everything they had, they didn't want to have to obey God or depend on God. They wanted to be equal to God. One thing that really bothered them was God told them they could not eat the fruit of a particular tree in the Garden; if they did they would die. That is a symbol too. It represents some very serious command God had given them. The story tells us about a tempter who came to them in the form of a snake. The tempter told them if they ate the forbidden fruit they would be like God. So they did. Right away they knew they had done wrong. They began to feel shame and guilt. Then they began to try to blame someone else for what they had done. Since there wasn't anyone else around whom they could blame, Adam blamed his wife and his wife blamed the serpent. God told them they had been warned and now they and the children they would have were going to lose most of the blessings he had given them. They would also struggle with the tempter all their lives (talking to the serpent God said: "From now on you and the woman will be enemies, and your offspring and

Fourth Sunday of Advent
December 18, 2011

INTRODUCTION – (2 Samuel 7: 1-5, 8b-12, 14a, 16; Luke 1:26-38) For the past three weeks of Advent we have been hearing Isaiah, John the Baptist, and Jesus tell us to stay awake, to be prepared for Jesus' coming, especially for his coming in the future. The last week before Christmas, our focus is primarily on the events that immediately preceded Jesus' birth. Three weeks ago I said most of our gospels this year are from St. Mark. But Mark's gospel begins with Jesus already an adult, so today we borrow from St. Luke's gospel the beautiful story of the Annunciation to Mary that she will be Jesus' mother. Our first reading today will help us have a greater understanding of the profound meaning in the Angel Gabriel's message to Mary. Our first reading goes back almost 1000 years before Jesus was born to the time of King David. David had recently conquered Jerusalem from the Jebusites, he made it the capital of his kingdom and it was there that he built himself a palace. But the Arc of the Covenant, which was the special sign of God's presence among God's people, was still being kept in a tent. Ever since Moses had constructed it according to God's command, 300 years before David, the Arc of the Covenant had been kept in a tent. David decided it deserved to be treated with greater honor so he told the prophet Nathan he would build a temple for God. The next day Nathan reports that God turned down David's proposal. That's where today's first reading comes in. God said David's son would build the Temple. However, God told David that he would build a house for David; i.e., God would establish David's dynasty so that one of his descendants would always reign as king. Amazingly, even after the northern tribes broke away after Solomon's death, David's kingdom lasted for 400 years in Judea. In 587 BC, when the Babylonians conquered the Jews, it put an end to the Davidic dynasty. But the Jews never forgot God's promise to David: "your house and your kingdom shall endure forever before me; your throne shall stand firm forever." This is an extremely important prophecy. For centuries the Jews expected that someone from David's descendants would rise up and re-establish the kingdom of David and rule once again in a free and independent Israel. In the gospel, we hear the Angel Gabriel announce to Mary that her son would fulfill this prophecy far beyond anyone's expectations. Mary's son would inherit "the throne of David his father, and he would rule over the house of Jacob forever and of his kingdom there would be no end."

HOMILY – When Jesus was born, Herod the Great had been king in Israel for almost 30 years. He would die about three years after Jesus' birth – although he must have thought he would live forever with his cowardly attempt to eliminate the "new born king of the Jews." Herod's father was an Idumean, that is an Edomite. He came from a country southeast of Judah which was forced into conversion to Judaism. Herod's mother was an Arabian princess, so he was half Jewish at best. Herod was half Jewish and half pagan in his religious observance too. Herod's father was a good politician and he trained his son well. Their efforts to gain favor with the Roman Emperor gained for each of them positions of leadership over the Jews. (Remember everyone in the Mediterranean area was under the Roman Emperor at that time). Herod was not at all popular among the Jews nor did they see him as their king (after all he was not of the House of David). Let us consider another king now, whose crown was made of thorns, not of gold. Central to

Jesus' teaching and ministry was God's kingdom, a kingdom that would eliminate suffering, sadness, injustice and even death. Jesus, without touting the fact that he was king and messiah, taught and acted in such manner as to show that he was the way into that kingdom. As Luke begins his gospel he tells us clearly, so we don't have to guess, who Jesus is: "he will inherit the throne of David his father, he will rule over the house of Jacob forever and of his kingdom there will be no end." Even more than a king who will reign forever, he will be Son of God. He will be conceived miraculously by God. Who would not want to listen to such a person and learn from him and follow him?

The Credo we say each week is a theological formulation of what the angel says so beautifully and this might be a good occasion to examine the Creed more closely. The Apostles Creed, one of the earliest of creeds, expresses these truths briefly. The Nicene Creed, written in 325, expresses them at greater length. These truths are spelled out fully because by 325 the Church had to deal with many erroneous beliefs about Jesus. For example, some groups, who believed that everything in the material world was evil, believed Jesus was divine, but not really human (he just looked human); at the other extreme, many thought he was human, but not quite divine. This is why the Church was so precise in its creed as to what we are to believe about Christ. (I want to mention three changes to the creed). First off we say, "I believe." This is still the faith of the Church, but it is the faith each of us individually professes. The expression parallels the Apostles Creed, the profession of faith each of us made at baptism or which someone made for us. A complaint I often hear is about the word "consubstantial." This is a new word for many people. I think it's a good thing to increase our vocabulary. It's not a difficult word to figure out. "Con" means "together" or "with" and "substantial" is related to the word "substance" which means, "what an entity is." So when we say Jesus is "not made" but is "consubstantial with the Father," we are saying we believe Jesus is of the same divine substance, he has the same essential being as the Father. He is like the Father in every way (as he said to Philip at the Last Supper: "he who sees me, sees the Father.") Yet Jesus is not the Father and that gets into the mystery of the Trinity (which we will explain some other time!). The word "consubstantial" is an attempt to describe something so unique: that Jesus is divine just as much as the Father is divine, and so we need a unique word to describe it. "Incarnate" is another word that is unusual for many people. Most of us are familiar with the word "reincarnation," which means living life all over again. Literally it means becoming flesh again because "carnis" means "flesh." We have that word in "carnal," "carnivorous," "carnage" and so on. So when we say "by the Holy Spirit (Jesus) was incarnate of the Virgin Mary," we are saying Jesus took his human nature from Mary, a mystery that came about by the power of the Holy Spirit. From that very instant that he took on human flesh he was God's Son. The Church opposes abortion for a similar reason. We argue that from the moment the spark of life begins in a mother-to-be, that life is human life and is worthy of being treated as a human being. At the very moment Jesus began to exist in Mary, he was divine Son of God as well as being human like us. We celebrate the incarnation of Jesus on March 25 – the feast of the Annunciation. Christmas is the result of Jesus taking on our human nature and of Mary's saying, "may it be done to me according to your word." It is an awesome mystery we believe in and which we are soon to celebrate. Amen.

Christmas
December 25, 2011

HOMILY – Each year in a Catholic grade school in Maryland the school had a Christmas pageant. The sixth grade students starred as the main characters. The key roles went to Joseph and Mary, of course. One particular girl in the school had her heart set on being the Blessed Virgin, but when she reached the sixth grade she was six inches taller than the tallest boy. The teacher in charge of the pageant didn't think it would look good so she broke the bad news to the girl that she couldn't be the Virgin Mary because she would be so much taller than St. Joseph. The girl excelled not only in height but also in wisdom. She told the teacher, "excuse me teacher, but if it didn't matter to Joseph that Mary was going to have a baby which was not his – do you think it mattered to him if she were taller than he was?" She got the role. (adapted from *Chicken Soup for the Soul, Christmas Magic*, pg 67)

We know from St. Matthew that Joseph did have a problem with marrying Mary and was about to back out of their engagement until an angel revealed to him that it was through the Holy Spirit that Mary was about to become a mother. We celebrate Jesus' birth today, a birth that was remarkable in many ways. The most remarkable part is that the Holy Spirit was so much a part of Jesus' birth. In addition to this most remarkable event, angels announced Jesus' birth beforehand, and angels announced his birth to shepherds after he was born. Not only was his birth remarkable but his public life was too: his powerful preaching, his exorcisms, healings, even raising people from the dead back to life. One of the most remarkable things people are often not aware of is that in a short time (probably about three years) he gathered a following around himself and began a movement that continues to grow. Others who began great spiritual movements worked at it for long periods of time: for example Buddha – 45 years, Mohammed – 22 years, Moses – 40 years (Jesus – 3 years). But the most remarkable things of all is that Jesus himself rose from the dead and sent his Spirit to guide and direct his followers. Other people in history have made claims to being divine, have had a reputation for being great teachers, were holy men and women, some even had miraculous powers. If it had not been for Jesus' resurrection and the power of the Holy Spirit, we would never have heard of Jesus. The Apostles would never have had the courage to spread his message. This remarkable man, Jesus the Messiah (the Christ), a man with little or no earthly power or influence has influenced millions of lives in the past 2000 years. Today we celebrate his birth; we celebrate the gift God gave us when he sent us Jesus. We celebrate with lights for he is the light of the world. We celebrate with music for he came to bring harmony and peace to the world. We celebrate with gifts for he is God's gift sent to us – God's only Son. We can never forget the reason why he was sent. He came down to us in order to lift us up, to make us sharers in God's life and to make us God's true sons and daughters, children of God who will be with God forever. That is what gives us hope in this world, hope in times of sadness and crisis, hope in times of war and chaos. God has great plans for us, greater than any of us are able to imagine. Jesus has come to lead us along the way that will bring us to the eternal happiness for which we were created. Christmas is more than the celebration of the birth of Jesus. In Christmas we are made aware of our own rebirth into eternal life which came through faith and baptism and which is nourished each week through the Eucharist. In union with this remarkable person, Jesus, who was born and died and has risen and is with us yet, we celebrate God's love and ask that someday we may celebrate that love forever in his kingdom. Amen.

Holy Family
December 29, 2002

INTRODUCTION – (Sirach 3:2-6, 12-14; Col 3:12-21; Luke 2:22-40) The Christmas season will last for two more weeks. With Joseph taking Mary as his wife and with the birth of Jesus, a new family is founded and it is a holy one. Ben Sirach, who speaks to us in today's first reading, was a teacher in a Jerusalem school nearly 200 years before Christ was born. Sirach's instructions cover topics such as home life, business, courtship and marriage, travel and entertainment. He even offers proper etiquette for entertaining guests or how to behave when invited out. Today's passage deals with our relationship with our parents, the importance of respect and obedience when we're young, and patience and kindness when we get older and they are too. In our second reading, Paul is writing to counteract the heretical teachings of those who thought that salvation was reserved only for those who were members of certain secret cults. He tells us it's the ordinary virtues that everyone knows and anyone can practice that are important; such as compassion, kindness, humility, gentleness, patience, forgiveness and love. Notice the importance he places on religious virtues such as familiarity with the word of God, prayer, singing and thanksgiving. The Greek word for thanksgiving is Eucharistia. When husbands hear Paul talk about wives being submissive to their husbands, they sometimes do not hear what follows. There is a mutual giving and receiving that is needed in marriage.

HOMILY – When the Holy Family is put before us as a model for us to imitate, we feel that is impossible. They are so far beyond us in holiness that imitating them would be like any of us trying to play baseball like Mickey Mantle or Babe Ruth. Well, we may not be the perfect holy family, but we are a holy family if we are in God's grace. It's God's grace that makes us holy and if the members of our family stay in God's grace, we are a holy family. The only danger we face is becoming spiritually complacent and lazy. We never stay in the same place spiritually, we are either moving forward or backward, and unless we keep trying to grow in God's grace, we will end up slipping backward or even losing grace altogether. As we heard in the second reading, there are no secrets to living and growing in grace. It's just a matter of practicing the ordinary virtues we learned when we were young: kindness, humility, gentleness, patience, etc. Jesus summed them up in his famous answer about the greatest commandment: loving God as much as we can and loving our neighbor as ourselves. The neighbor that we most often neglect is the person or persons closest to us. We too often take each other for granted instead of making time for one another, helping each other, complimenting each other, thanking each other or being patient and forgiving of one another. Good relationships are made up of just so many little things.

I think at times we imagine the Holy Family lived a charmed life without problems or stress. Problems began even before Jesus was born when Joseph was about to break his engagement to Mary. Think for a moment where Jesus was born – not neat and clean like the little mangers we put up in our homes. He was born in a stable that probably was smelly and dirty, maybe damp and cold. In today's gospel we are told about their presenting Jesus in the Temple and offering the required sacrifice according to the law of the Lord. St. Luke is telling us they were poor, they offered the sacrifice of the poor. St. Luke, incidentally, is telling us they observed the laws of their Jewish faith and were obedient to God. We can't be holy and ignore the things God asks of us. As they went to the Temple, surely they were happy to be able to bring their child there. But then an old man came up to tell Mary her heart would some day be broken because of her child. What a chilling prophecy! Shortly after this St. Joseph is told by an angel to get out of the area, that the king is planning on killing their child. So they end up refugees in a foreign land for a few years. The only other event we know of during Jesus' youth was when he was 12 and he was lost in the Temple for three days.

What a worry and concern that must have been. A holy family is not a family without problems or heart aches. It's how we deal with those problems that really matters. We must be faithful to God at all times and we must deal with each other with fairness, kindness, patience and love. May God's blessings be with you and your families today and throughout the coming year.

Mary Mother of God
January 1, 2012

HOMILY – (Num 6:22-27; Gal 4:4-7; Luke 2:16-21) I usually try to write a fresh homily every Sunday, one that's not yet been printed in any of my books, but as I looked back over homilies I have preached on this date, I found one that I thought was interesting enough to repeat. We celebrate New Year's Day today, and most countries in the world do, but not everyone. Many cultures have their own New Year's Day. For example, the Jewish new year begins on Rosh Hashanah which will begin this year at sunset on September 16, 2012, and lasts until nightfall on the 18th (two full days) (that would give you a good hangover). Back in 1990, I was in Israel on Rosh Hashanah at the Wailing Wall, the place where the Temple stood before the Romans destroyed it in 70 AD and I witnessed the rabbis blowing of rams' horns to start their New Year. The Chinese have their own New Year celebration, which will be on Jan. 23 of 2012. It will begin the year of the dragon. The Moslem New Year began on Nov. 26, 2011. Their next New Year will be Nov. 14, 2012. Their year is 11 to 12 days shorter than ours. We tend to think everyone in the world should think the way we do. There are many other cultures who celebrate their own new year at times and seasons different than we do. January 1 was chosen as the start of the New Year by the early Romans in 153 BC. Prior to that date, they celebrated the New Year in the spring which has a certain logic to it since winter is over and nature starts to come alive at that time. In 153 BC the Roman senate chose January 1 as the beginning of a new year because that was the day when the Roman consuls took office. (Maybe they used the start of the New Year to give themselves an increase in salary and they didn't have to wait three months until the beginning of spring to start their salary.) It is said they celebrated with "boisterous joy, superstitious practices and gross orgies." The early Christians made January 1 a day of penance as a reaction against the excesses of the pagans. Eventually Christians designated January 1 as the first feast in the Church calendar dedicated to Mary, Jesus' mother. Incidentally, many European countries didn't officially make January 1 the start of the new year until the 16th, 17th, and 18th centuries. Now practically all big cities of the world celebrate on January 1 even if they have their own new year, like China.

The Church calendar begins a new liturgical year on the first Sunday of Advent. For the Church January 1 presents us with several themes. It is first of all the octave of Christmas. Christmas is too important a feast for just a one-day celebration, so the liturgy celebrates Christmas solemnly for eight days. After today, the liturgy continues to celebrate Christmas, but less solemnly, until the feast of the Baptism of our Lord which this year is on Monday, January 9th, the day after the feast of the Epiphany. Today also recalls the circumcision of Jesus, which traditionally took place for a Jewish boy on the eighth day after birth. It's also the day on which a child was officially named – although both Joseph and Mary were told ahead of time by an angel that his name would be Jesus – a name which means "God saves." On this day we might reflect for a moment how respectful we are of this name by which we are to be saved. For many years now the popes have designated this day as a day of prayer for peace, which is so badly needed in today's world.

There are a lot of reasons to gather in prayer today. A new year begins new opportunities to grow in God's grace and favor, new opportunities to learn, new opportunities to discover ways to treat the ills we suffer from, new ways to heal from what we have lost in the past, new ways, hopefully, to create a world in which the poor are fed and in which we can all live together in peace. I might mention that today is an anniversary for our own parish too. On December 29, 20 years ago, St. Boniface and St. Patrick's parishes merged. It is something the people of our two parishes can be proud of that the merger went so well. This new year gives us new opportunities to prosper and grow and serve the members of our parish and to share God's word with our neighbors in Northside. We also honor Mary, the Mother of God, in this, the most ancient feast of Mary in the Church calendar. We ask her to intercede for us that this may be a blessed year for all of us. Amen.

Feast of the Epiphany
January 4, 2009

INTRODUCTION – (Isaiah 60:1-6; Eph 3:2-3a, 5-6; Matt 2:1-12) 587 years before Christ, Jerusalem was destroyed by the Babylonians. Fifty years later, the Persians (people living in modern day Iran) conquered the Babylonians, and they allowed the Jews to return home. It was a difficult time for the Jews, rebuilding their country 50 years after it had been destroyed. Their Temple was gone. Jerusalem, their city that gave them such pride, was in shambles. The prophet in today's first reading tries to encourage the people and assures them Jerusalem would again be a great city. He sees Jerusalem becoming a light for all the world. People would come from everywhere to visit Jerusalem and to be nourished by the radiant light of God's presence. St. Matthew sees the vision of the prophet fulfilled in the birth of Jesus and the visit of the magi.

HOMILY – There are so many lessons we can learn from the story of the magi. I am going to dwell on only two of them. They are themes that are very dear to St. Matthew's gospel and I want to spend a few moments showing how these themes appear again and again in his gospel. First is the theme that God wants all people to be saved. The Jews, as God's chosen people, believed they had a monopoly on salvation. The magi were foreigners, not members of God's chosen people, but they represent all nations whom God calls to know him through Jesus. As we read further on in Matthew's gospel we see how this theme is repeated. Although Jesus instructed his apostles not to go into pagan territory when he sent them out to preach, Jesus himself did not hesitate to cure the servant of a pagan, a Roman centurion. He even marveled at the centurian's faith and on that occasion remarked that "many will come from the east and the west and will recline with Abraham, Isaac, and Jacob at the banquet in the kingdom of heaven" while many of the "chosen people" would miss out. In another place he cured the daughter of a Canaanite woman after he challenged her faith. But most of all, the theme of universal salvation comes through clearly in St. Matthew's gospel when Jesus is about to ascend into heaven. He tells his apostles "Go, therefore, and make disciples of all nations, baptizing them in the name of the Father, and of the Son and of the Holy Spirit, teaching them to observe all I have commanded you."

The visit of the magi tells us God has opened up the doors of salvation to all people, but, and this is the second theme, not everyone chooses to enter into God's kingdom. The story of the magi tells us we have to put some energy and time into finding God and entering into eternal life. Entrance into God's eternal kingdom doesn't come automatically. It doesn't even come if we know our religion perfectly but don't live it. The magi came quite a distance, hundreds of miles, probably even over a thousand, to find Jesus. They had to keep searching, even seeking help from the paranoid king Herod and the indifferent Jewish clergy who had all the answers, but not enough interest in finding the messiah themselves. God's kingdom is for everyone, but not everyone comes looking for it and only those who do, find it. It is a theme we find repeated in many of the teachings of Jesus in St. Matthew's gospel. For example, at the end of the Sermon on the Mount, Jesus tells us the person who listens to his words and acts on them is like a person who builds his house on rock, whereas a person who listens to his words but does not act on them is like the person who builds his house on sand. It will end up in ruins. The theme is repeated in a number of parables. Here's eight that come to mind immediately: 1) the sower and the seed, 2) the wheat and the weeds, 3) the buried treasure and the pearl of great price, 4) the parable about two sons, one who told his father he would do the work his father asked of him but didn't and the other who said he wouldn't, but did, 5) the wedding feast where those invited were too busy to come, 6) the parable of the talents where one man didn't do anything with his talent and lost it in the end, 7) the ten virgins, five of whom were prepared when the groom arrived, and five who missed out on the wedding feast because they were not ready for the groom's arrival. 8) Matthew is the only gospel who gives us the parable of the last judgment when those who were kind and good to the needy were rewarded while those who weren't were rejected from the kingdom.

God's word is absolutely contradicted by our modern day culture, which tells us everyone somehow is going to make it into heaven. The story of the magi shows us those who sincerely search for Christ will find him, but unfortunately not everyone is interested in searching for him sincerely. We ask him today to help us not to get lazy or discouraged as we continue seeking him. His light and grace will always guide us. If we faithfully follow that light, we can be confident we will be saved for Christ for he came a long way to find us and suffered much in order to do so. We recall his saving love as we continue our Mass. Amen.

Baptism of the Lord
January 11, 2009

INTRODUCTION – (Isaiah 55:1-11; 1 John 5:1-9; Mark 1:7-11) Many kings, prophets, and holy people served God in Old Testament times, but in four places in the book of the prophet Isaiah, God speaks of someone with whom he is especially pleased. This servant is not identified by name, and because the passages are in poetic form, they are usually referred to as the servant songs. They were written about 500 years before Christ. Perhaps the passages refer to someone who was alive at the time of the prophet but, amazingly, although they were written 500 years before the time of Christ, they describe Jesus so perfectly. At Jesus' baptism, the voice of God is heard, introducing Jesus to the world, as not only his servant, but as his beloved Son.

HOMILY – Today we celebrate the feast of the Baptism of our Lord. Even though it is an event that took place roughly 30 years after Jesus' birth and the coming of the Magi, it is a feast that fits with the theme of Epiphany. Epiphany means to cause something to be seen, to show, to illuminate or manifest. In last week's feast God revealed his son to the world as represented by the magi. God again reveals his son at the baptism by John the Baptist with his declaration from heaven: "You are my beloved son; with you I am well pleased." So, if you think we are a little slow about removing our Christmas decorations, they are still appropriate to the season. On Monday, Ordinary time begins. It is then that the Christmas/Epiphany season is over. Since they are still so beautiful, we may keep a few poinsettia's around for another week or so. John's baptism was a baptism of repentance. It's hard for us to understand why Jesus, the sinless one, God's Son, came to John for a baptism of repentance. Even John the Baptist had difficulty understanding why Jesus came to him for baptism. As John said "I need to be baptized by you, and yet you are coming to me?" Because it is difficult to understand, various explanations have been offered as to why Jesus was baptized.

1) Some of the early Church Fathers said Jesus went into the water of the Jordan, not in order to be made holy, but to make the water holy so that all the waters of the world would become life giving through the sacrament of baptism.

2) It crossed my mind that another possible reason Jesus went to be baptized was to show us what his baptism would do, that his baptism would bring the Spirit down upon us and we would become God's beloved children.

3) Inauguration is on everyone's mind these days. Perhaps we can see Jesus' baptism as his official inauguration as he began the work the Father had given him. He was ready to proclaim the gospel, the good news, that for those who turned their hearts to God, God's Kingdom was there for them. The Father and the Spirit put their approval on him and would guide him in this ministry to the world.

4) The last possible explanation I have is perhaps Jesus went to be baptized as an example to us that we are to be baptized in order to become God's sons and daughters. Right before Jesus ascended into heaven he sent his apostles to continue his work (and that by the way is what the word "apostle" means: one who has been sent). He told them: "All power in heaven and on earth has been given to me. Go, therefore, and make disciples of all nations, baptizing them in the name of the Father, and of the Son, and of the Holy Spirit, teaching them to

observe all that I have commanded you. And behold, I am with you always, until the end of the age." If these were his last words, as St. Matthew tells us, baptism must be really important to our Lord. Most of us do not remember our baptism. We don't remember most of the things that happened to us in our earliest year. Yet those are the things that gave direction to our lives: how we were to treat others, what kinds of food we were to eat, how to care for ourselves, how to act in public, how we were to be educated. In taking us for baptism our parents were setting a direction for us, setting us on the path to holiness through faith in Jesus Christ. Sometimes parents take their child for baptism because they think they should, but they fail to see the life of Christ that baptism gives has to be nourished and to have opportunity to grow. You might have heard the story about the family who took their second child to church for baptism and after the baptism the older child who was three years old sobbed all the way back home.

His father asked what was wrong. He said, "the priest said he wanted us to be brought up in a Christian home and I want to stay with you guys." Baptism gives Christ's life, a life that needs to be nurtured and given the opportunity to grow just like the baby's physical life does. Some more fundamental religions say let the child grow up and get baptized when they're older so they can make their own choice as to what religion they want to belong to. Parents don't do that with anything else that's important. They don't say we won't send you to school and when you're old enough you can decide what you need to learn; or we'll let you eat whatever you want until you're old enough to decided for yourself. Baptism gives God's life and sets the direction for that life. The child, when he or she is grown, will have to make his or her own choice as to if and how much he or she will be faithful to Christ. When they see their children begin to drift away, that's when a lot of parents do some heavy praying. If this happens, don't give up hope for them and don't stop praying. I feel as if my thoughts have drifted in various directions and I know much more could be said about baptism. I just want to leave you with one thought. Even though most of us may not remember our baptism, we should thank God, for in it he gave us life and the Spirit and he gave us a loving parent or parents to guide us in the ways of God.

Second Sunday Ordinary Time
January 15, 2012

INTRODUCTION – (1 Sam 3:3b-10, 19; 1 Cor 6:13-15, 17-20; John 1:35-42) Today's first reading is about Samuel who lived a little more than 1000 years before Christ. Samuel was a person of major importance in the Old Testament. He was a great prophet, he anointed King Saul as Israel's first king, and later he anointed David to be king. He had an unbelievable influence over the religious and political climate of his day and for many centuries thereafter. At the beginning of the book of Samuel, we are told that his mother, Hannah, was unable to have children; she suffered bitterly over that fact. She constantly prayed for a son; she promised God if she had a son she would dedicate him to God's service. God heard her prayer. When Samuel was still a young child, Hanna brought him to the High Priest, Eli. Eli cared for the Arc of the Covenant, and he raised Samuel to assist him in his service to God. This will give some background to today's first reading.

HOMILY – I think we have been doing very well here at St. Boniface in accepting and adjusting to the new translation of the prayers of the Mass. Some of the translations I personally find a little awkward, but on the whole I feel very comfortable with most of the prayers and I feel they are very beautifully worded. I promised I would do some more explanation of the changes, and today's readings gives me that opportunity. John the Baptist points to Jesus as the "Lamb of God." The idea of sacrifice is written all over that expression. The Greek word used here for "lamb" (amnos) does not mean just any lamb. It means a one year-old lamb without blemish. That was the only kind of lamb that could be offered to God in sacrifice. We all know that at Passover time a lamb was sacrificed and it became the centerpiece of the Passover meal for each Jewish family. St. John's gospel refers to this sacrifice of the Paschal lamb, which took place about noon on the preparation day for Passover. John tells us this was the exact time that Pilate sentenced Jesus to death. The Lamb of God would be sacrificed at the same time the Passover lamb was being sacrificed. But lambs were not only sacrificed at Passover. Every day throughout the year, two lambs were sacrificed in the Temple as a morning and evening offering. At other times, a lamb was offered as a sin offering, as an offering of praise and adoration, as a thanksgiving sacrifice or as a request for some favor from God. It was always a one year-old lamb without blemish. Why a lamb? Sheep were a major part of the Jewish life. From sheep the Jews got wool for clothes, meat (on special occasions) and milk and they found other uses for sheep's skin and horns such as for tents and writing material. But what kind of a gift is this that we give God. He made everything there is. The only thing we can really give him is ourselves. Since we can't just lie down and die, we offer something that represents value to us; we offer something that symbolizes our life; we don't offer some meaningless object that we could just as easily throw away. God can see in our heart how meaningful are our offerings of love or praise or repentance. In the course of time, the sacrifices of lambs and calves and wine and oil and cereal offerings was to be replaced by a more perfect sacrifice, offered by one who would represent the whole human race, one who would offer perfect love to the Heavenly Father. This one's sacrifice would put an end to all other sacrifices for it would be perfect not just momentarily but forever. Each person could make this one perfect sacrifice their own when they wanted to approach the Father with praise or love or repentance or petitioning a favor for Paul tells us today, "whoever is joined to the Lord becomes one Spirit with him." No greater sacrifice can be offered to God than the Lamb of God. We praise Jesus as the Lamb of God in the Gloria. At the Passover supper, when the Jewish family ate the Paschal lamb that had been sacrificed they knew they were eating sacred food, they pictured themselves eating and drinking with God. Later on in the Mass, as we prepare to participate in Jesus' sacrifice by eating of the sacred food he offers us, we say or sing the Agnus Dei, the Lamb of God, and we ask him to have mercy on us and to bring us peace. Then the priest holds up the Eucharist and says, "Behold the Lamb of God, behold him who takes away the sins of the world. Blessed are those called to the supper of the Lamb." It is truly the supper of the Lamb because Jesus becomes our food and our drink. But this supper looks to future glory as well. In the Book of Revelation (19:9), there is a brief mention of the supper of the Lamb being a marriage celebration. It is not described for it is too awesome to describe. Isaiah gives us a hint of it when he tells us that in the heavenly Jerusalem, God would provide for all peoples a feast of rich food and choice wines, juicy rich food and pure choice wines; God would destroy death forever and wipe away the tears from all faces. (Is. 25:6ff) Jesus gives us a hint of it in one of his parables about a king who gave a wedding feast for his son. Can you imagine what an elaborate affair that would be? (Mt. 22:1ff) Many people watched on TV the wedding of Prince William and Kate Middleton. The wedding feast in Jesus' parable would have matched that and more since weddings at Jesus' time went on for a few days. (That's why they ran out of wine in Cana, but Jesus solved that problem. They won't run out in heaven.) Pope John Paul encouraged us to nourish ourselves with this Eucharistic Bread for it will sustain us and support our faith for as he said: "only he who perseveres will be worthy to share in the marriage supper of the Lamb." (Radio message, July 22, 1984) (from *The Navarre Bible: Revelation*, pg 135) After the priest proclaims the Eucharist to be the Lamb of God, the people respond with a passage from Matthew 8:8 where Jesus was asked to heal the servant of a Roman centurion (a Gentile). Jesus said he would come and cure the sick person. It was forbidden for Jews to enter a Gentile home and the centurion was sensitive to that. He answered, "Lord, I am not worthy to have you enter under my roof; only say the word and my servant will be healed."

As you can see there is a lot in this little phrase: "The Lamb of God." And much more could be said. The Church, along with John the Baptist, points to Jesus today as our sacrifice, our perfect gift we can offer God as we unite ourselves with Christ's sacrifice. It is the greatest prayer we can offer. It is the greatest gift God can offer us, his presence with us, his Word to us and himself in Holy Communion. Before leaving Mass today, see if you can notice the image of the lamb on our high altar. It is Jesus represented as a lamb in the Book of

Revelation, the only one who could open the scroll that was sealed with seven seals and which revealed the future of the world. Amen.

Third Sunday Ordinary Time
January 22, 2012

INTRODUCTION – (Jonah 3:1-5, 10; 1 Cor 7:29-31; Mark 1:14-20) Whenever we think of Jonah, we think of his being swallowed whole by a great fish (the Bible makes no mention of a whale). The story of how he was swallowed by a fish is a long one, but basically he was trying to escape from the mission God gave him to preach repentance to the Assyrians. You need to know that the Assyrians were an especially warlike, aggressive, merciless people who lived on the Tigris River, 250 miles north of Baghdad. The Assyrians had already destroyed most of Israel by the time Jonah was written, so you can imagine there was deep hatred on the part of the Jews for the Assyrians. Jonah was three days in the belly of the fish before he was spit out on the shore of Assyria. Having learned he couldn't run away from God, Jonah decided he had better do what God wanted. The story about Jonah that we hear in our first reading today is more amazing than the part of the story about the fish. Without miracles or spectacular signs, Jonah proclaimed, unenthusiastically, a one-line warning to the people of Nineveh. In one day the entire city of Nineveh was converted. To get an idea of how astonishing this would be, think of an unknown individual showing up in Baghdad today, and in one day, every person, including all the terrorists, repenting and converting to Christianity. Would that be something or what!!! Today's reading shows God is not interested in punishing people but in giving all people, even the bad guys, a chance to reform. The passage sets the theme for the gospel when Jesus began his public ministry by preaching repentance. We know from real life experience and from the experience Jesus and the Apostles had, calling people to change their lives is not as easy as the story of Jonah makes it appear to be.

HOMILY – A little girl was sitting on her grandfather's lap as he read her a bedtime story. From time to time she would reach up and touch his wrinkled cheek, then she would feel her own. Finally she asked, "Grandpa, did God make you?" "Yes, sweetie," he said, "a long time ago." Then she asked, "did God make me too?" "Yes, sweetheart," he answered, just a short time ago." Feeling his face and hers she observed, "God's getting better at it, isn't he?" Today St. Paul tells us "the time is running out. The world in its present form is passing away." When we are young we never think we will be old. But if we are fortunate it happens. Paul is telling us to use the time we have wisely. In Paul's mind that means to put God's kingdom before everything else. That's what Jesus is telling us in today's gospel too. "This is the time of fulfillment. The kingdom of God is at hand." This is Jesus' message as he begins his ministry: the kingdom is at hand. It's not a place he is talking about, but something dynamic and active. It is God's rule over us, a rule that is something good – this is good news Jesus proclaims. It's good news because the God who reigns over us is not a fearsome, autocratic, authoritarian tyrant, but a father, a father who wants to share his love with all his children.

We can get lost in the kingdom of this world, attracted by its pleasures, depressed by its tragedies. None of it will last for a new kingdom, a new way of seeing, a new way of living is breaking into the world as we have come to know it. This theme on the kingdom is central to Jesus' ministry. He shows us by his exorcisms that there is no place for evil in the kingdom he announces; he shows us by his miracles that sickness and suffering will be eliminated; he feeds the multitude to show us no one will ever suffer from hunger; he uses parables to help us grasp what God's kingdom will be like; he shows us by raising people back to life and especially by his own resurrection that even death will be done away with. It's something different than the world has ever known. That's why he calls us to repent. It's a word that means change. Change our mind, change our hearts, change our viewpoint, change the direction of our lives, change our values: that is put his kingdom first. "Seek first the kingdom of God and his righteousness" (Mt. 6:33) Everything else is secondary. We have to live in this world, we have to use the things of this world, we have to have clothes, food, warmth, a place to live, friends to support us, these are all necessary, but as Paul tells us today we must use the world as not using it fully." (1 Cor. 7:31) That means living in this world and NOT using it as if that's all that's important to me. "Seek first the kingdom of God and all these things will be given to you besides." (Mt. 6:33)

Getting this message out to everyone was a big job, and so we hear in today's gospel Jesus calling on others to help him. Jesus continues to need people to help him share his good news. At the request of the Archbishop, we pray at the end of each Mass that there will be enough people to step forward to help bring about the kingdom Jesus announced.

The reason we are here at Mass today is because we believe in Christ. Unless there's a St. Francis among us, I suspect there is room for improvement in all of us. Jesus' call to conversion is sort of like New Year's resolutions. We make New Year's resolutions because we realize we can do better; we can be better; we have more potential than we are using.

Until we hopefully reach heaven where we will be perfect, there'll always be room for improvement, always some areas of our lives where we could be more fully dedicated to the kingdom. Would that conversion were as easy as the book of Jonah pictures it. If it were, we wouldn't have to be reminded of it so often. Amen.

Fourth Sunday Ordinary Time
January 29, 2012

INTRODUCTION – (Deut 18:15-20; 1 Cor. 7:32-35; Mark 1:21-28) Our second reading from Paul's letter to the Corinthians might be difficult to understand. So I would like to give a little background. The passage comes from a section of the letter where Paul replies to several questions he received in a letter from the Corinthians. In today's reading he is dealing with a question about marriage and celibacy. Paul begins by affirming the value of marriage and then he moves on, which is today's reading, to affirm the value of celibacy. He is not making a rule, but a suggestion to those who were not yet married or who were widowed and he points out the advantages of remaining in such a state (i.e. unmarried). Behind this suggestion was the expectation of the early Church, including Paul, that Jesus was going to return very soon and with his coming the world would come to an end. To quote what Paul said in last week's reading: "the time is running out" and "the world as we know it is passing away." If it sounds as if Paul is overemphasizing the spiritual advantages of celibacy, consider how you might view things with regard to getting married and starting a family if you seriously thought that probably in a year or three the world would end and Jesus would return.

Some background about our first reading might also be helpful. The setting is on the East side of the Jordan River across from the Promised Land. After many years in the desert, God's people were ready to cross the Jordan and enter a land flowing with milk and honey. Moses knew that God was calling him to leave this world and God's people would cross the Jordan and enter the Promised Land without him. Basically he is saying "goodbye." He assures them God would not leave them without direction or leadership. God would send them another prophet like himself who would speak God's word to them. We usually think of a prophet as a person who foretells the future and sometimes the prophet did, but the best definition of a prophet is at the end of today's first reading: one who speaks God's word. Our first reading prepares us for the gospel where Jesus speaks God's word with power and authority.

HOMILY – I believe that Jesus' experience with demons was also real. I would grant that probably in many situations epilepsy or mental illness were considered to be caused by demons, but I believe in other cases, it was the real thing Jesus was fighting against. Exorcisms make up the largest single category of healings in the gospels of Matthew, Mark and Luke. If in some cases Jesus was dealing with mental illness or epilepsy, we need to remember Jesus was a Jew who lived two thousand years ago. He was a man of his times and he saw his job was to do battle with evil, whether it was an evil spirit or the evil of disease. We, as his followers, try to make the world a better place and eliminate evil to the extent that we can. I would like to particularly speak about a great evil today – the evil of abortion. All priests received a letter this week from the Archbishop asking us to publicize a major threat to our belief in the sanctity of life. I have put a copy of his letter as an insert in today's bulletin, (on one side of the blue sheet – on the other side are the results of our Thanksgiving festival). I want to read a couple of items from the Archbishop's letter. He said, "The U.S. Department of Health and Human Services announced last week that almost all employers, including Catholic employers, will be forced to offer their employees health coverage that includes sterilization, abortion–inducing drugs, and contraception. Almost all health insurers will be forced to include those "services" in the health policies they write. And almost all individuals will be forced to buy that coverage as a part of their policies And as a result, unless the rule is overturned, we Catholics will be compelled to violate our consciences, or to drop health coverage for our employees (and suffer the penalties for doing so)." The Archbishop, at the end of his letter, is asking two things of us: 1) to fast and pray that wisdom and justice may prevail and religious liberty may be restored. 2) to visit the web (the address is in his letter), to learn more about this severe assault on religious liberty, and how to contact Congress in support of legislation that would reverse the Administration's decision.

You may have heard this before, but consider the following three situations:

1) A preacher and his wife are very poor and almost destitute. They already have 14 children when she finds out she's pregnant with the 15th. Considering their impoverished status and the excessive global population, should an abortion be recommended?

2) A father is sick. The mother has tuberculosis. They have four children. The oldest is blind, the second has already died, the third is deaf, and the fourth also has

TB. The mother is pregnant again. Should an abortion be recommended?

3) A young, unmarried teenager becomes pregnant, greatly shaming her family. Although she recently got engaged, her finance is not the father of the baby, and he's beside himself with grief and anger. Should an abortion be recommended?

If you said yes to the first case, John Wesley, one of the greatest evangelists of the 19th century would have been aborted. In the second case, Beethoven. In the third case it would have been Jesus Christ himself.

The so called "pro-choice" people (who ironically do not consider whether the infant might have a choice in the matter of whether it lives or dies) say: "it's uncertain when human life begins. That's a religious question." Well it's scientific too. The DNA in a fertilized ovum shows the zygote is not that of a tree or a chicken or a chimpanzee or any other living thing except that of a human. Some say it doesn't look like a human. The question is what should a human look like? Does a male look like a female, does a Englishman look like an African, does a one year-old look like a fifteen year-old? Does a fifteen year old look like a fifty year-old? A fertilized ovum looks exactly like a human being ought to look at that stage of development! Killing a defenseless, innocent human being is a great evil! Multiply that by the incidence of this taking place, by 3,288 per day (stat from 2009), and we have to be astounded at how much evil our country is guilty of. We who hold life is sacred should not be forced into supporting such horrendous evil. Edmund Burke is credited with having said: "the only thing necessary for the triumph of evil is for good men to do nothing."

Fifth Sunday in Ordinary Time
February 5, 2012

INTRODUCTION – (Job 7:1-4, 6-7; 1 Cor 9:16-19, 22-23; Mark 1:29-39) We hear from Job in our first reading. He was prosperous and happy. Then suddenly he lost everything; hostile tribes destroyed his cattle, his sheep, his camels and his workers. A violent wind collapsed the house where his children were gathered for a meal and it killed them all at once. Soon after Job's health began to deteriorate and his skin was covered with sores. He was not a happy guy as he laments: "I shall not see happiness again." Job, who was always faithful to God, complained God was being unfair to him. At the time this book was written, God's people believed that if we are good, all will go well, and if we're not, all kinds of terrible things will happen to us. At the same time they were beginning to discover that life doesn't always work that way. Like Job we still struggle to answer the question of why good people suffer? The gospel is in contrast with the pathetic story of Job where we see Jesus at work trying to lessen people's sufferings by his many exorcisms and healings.

Contrary to Job who is deeply depressed, St. Paul, in today's second reading, is full of enthusiasm with his ministry of preaching the gospel. He's not doing it because he wants to get rich (actually, for the most part he provided for his own needs, working as a tentmaker). He is using himself as an example for the Corinthians to follow in teaching them to unselfishly serve God and lovingly serve one another.

HOMILY – I want to talk mostly of the picture St. Mark gives us of a day in the life of Jesus. It is a busy day as we will see. I will stick to this topic except for a brief theological digression. So first we start with this "eventful day" in the life of Jesus. It is told with some details suggesting this comes from the recollection of an eyewitness. The "eventful day" began with last Sunday's gospel with Jesus at synagogue in Capernaum on the Sabbath. He was teaching there. A man in the congregation, who was possessed by an unclean spirit, challenged Jesus for being there and Jesus, with a simple command, expelled the demon. Today's gospel continues on with Jesus going to the home of Peter and Andrew after the service was over. There has been some archeological work in Capernaum which gives us a picture of how people lived then. I remember being at the spot where the synagogue once stood where Jesus taught. Nothing is left of it now except the foundation. Nearby was the home of Peter. It was part of a complex of about five small dwellings connected together, gathered around a courtyard, that would have housed related families. Living in that complex would be uncles, aunts, children, grandparents, cousins, etc. It may seem fanciful to imagine that people have identified where Peter lived, but it is well supported that this was the home of Peter because one particular room has been venerated and preserved as Peter's home since the mid first century. Most probably Peter and Andrew were bringing Jesus to where they lived to get something to eat. But Peter's mother in law, probably the main cook, was sick. One can assume that Peter was married at the time of his call. There is a passage in Paul's letter to the Corinthians (1 Cor. 9:5) that suggests that his wife accompanied him on his apostolic journeys. That Peter's mother-in-law got up immediately and waited on them shows that Jesus' healing was effective.

Since this was still the Sabbath, it was not until evening, after sunset, when the neighbors could bring to

Jesus many who were sick or possessed. (To transport them during the Sabbath would have been an offense against the Law.) In the Jewish culture the day ends at sunset and a new day begins (just as we end our day at midnight and begin the next day at that time.) So the Sabbath was over when the sun set and people could bring the sick to Jesus. Mark said he cured many whereas Matthew said he cured them all. The meaning is the same (Mark means that there were many and he cured them.)

Now a theological digression. You might have noticed that when the priest consecrates the wine during Mass, he says "this is the chalice of my blood, the blood of the new and eternal covenant, which will be poured out for you and for many for the forgiveness of sins." It used to say "it will be shed for you and for all so that sins may be forgiven." This change has troubled some people. The original Greek uses the word "many" which our theology teaches us means everyone. Paul says it clearly in 2 Cor. (5:14-15) If some people are troubled by the use of the word "many" in the consecration of the wine, because they fear that implies that some people will not benefit from Christ's saving death, they should be especially troubled by a number of parables where Christ clearly teaches that many will not enjoy the blessing of his saving death, through their own choice, for the invitation into his kingdom has been offered to all, but not everyone chooses to respond.

Back to Mark's story, the next morning, Jesus is up before anyone else and goes off to a quiet place to pray. Notice how important prayer was to him. He needed to gain strength from his Heavenly Father, as we all do, in order to deal with everyday challenges.

To save all people, which is God's desire ("God wants all people to be saved" according to Paul (1 Timothy

2:4)), Jesus knew he couldn't just settle down in Capernaum to teach and heal and cast out demons. So he moved on, and he continues to move on today, offering eternal life to anyone who chooses to believe in him and follow him. That's what brings us here today. We believe he is the way to God, so in faith we offer him our love and ask him to walk with us as we make our journey through life. Amen.

Sixth Sunday in Ordinary Time
February 12, 2012

INTRODUCTION – (Lv 13:1-2, 44-46; 1 Cor 10:31-11:1; Mark 1:40-45) Our first reading is from the Book of Leviticus, the third book in the Bible. The name Leviticus is mostly made up of instructions for the levitical priesthood. There are many rules about feast days, fast days, worship, sacrifice and ordination. When people decide they are going to read the Bible from beginning to end, they usually give up their good intention to do so when they start reading Leviticus because it is page after page of Jewish law. There is a section on legal purity meaning who is allowed to participate in public worship. Two full chapters deal with how to deal with "leprosy." Our first reading today is a tiny passage taken from one of these chapters. Without the sophistication of modern medicine, the term "leprosy" was applied to almost any kind of skin disease: such as ringworm, psoriasis, eczema and leprosy itself. Anyone so afflicted with such diseases was required to avoid contact with anyone else lest the disease spread to the whole community. A "leper" could not work, go to synagogue or temple or even visit his or her family. Usually a "leper" ended up living in caves or tombs, alone or with other "lepers." It was the priest's job to decide when a person was disease-free and allow that person to re-enter society. Our first reading connects to the gospel which tells us about Jesus healing a "leper."

HOMILY – If you or I had happened to be with Jesus at the time this leper came up to him, we would have been shocked. The leper broke the rules coming up to Jesus and the disciples who most probably were with him. He should have stood at a distance and warned them not to come any nearer. Yet he came right up to Jesus and knelt down before him. The law would have forbidden any contact with the leper, yet Jesus touched him. That contact would have made Jesus legally unclean; however, instead it made the leper clean and it happened "immediately." Notice Jesus did not show any indication of disgust or offence, rather Jesus felt sorry for the man as Mark tells us.

I cannot read this gospel without thinking of St. Francis. There was a colony of lepers near Assisi. One of Francis' major life-changing events was to be approached by a leper begging alms. Francis felt repulse for the lepers; he would turn his head so he didn't have to see them and hold his nose because they gave off a terrible stench. However, shortly after Francis began to seek God, when the leper approached him Francis gave the man alms and kissed his hand. Then, with his disfigured face, the leper looked at Francis and the leper lifted his hands for the kiss of peace (which would have been an embrace). Francis could have run away, and there would have been plenty of reason to do so, but instead Francis embraced the leper, whose sores were oozing with pus, and kissed him. Francis, in his Testament, a document he dictated before he died, said of this event: "what seemed to me as bitter was transformed into sweetness of the soul and the body." After that encounter Francis was no longer the same person. Francis did not heal the leper as Jesus did, on the contrary, the leper seems to have healed Francis of any last shred of egoism or self-centeredness. Unlike in today's gospel, God did not remove the suffering of the leper, but the suffering of the leper helped God to create a great saint in Francis, a saint who has touched many millions.

In our gospel today, Jesus told the man he healed not to tell anyone else what Jesus had done. We find this often in the gospels, especially Mark, where Jesus does not want people to know about his miracles. Scripture scholars refer to this as the Messianic secret. Why would Jesus command this secrecy? Perhaps for a practical reason; as we hear in today's gospel, Jesus and his disciples had no time to themselves. But there is a deeper reason that is often given, Jesus didn't want people to see him merely as an exorcist or healer or a person who could calm a storm or feed a multitude. If that's what they thought he was all about, then they would have expected him to raise an army and expel the Romans from their land. That is not the kind of Messiah he was. His mission involved saving God's people through his suffering. Once when he predicted his sufferings, Peter protested that Jesus, the Messiah, would never have to suffer. As with other predictions, the apostles didn't get the message. So with Jesus knowledge of what was ahead he decided that he had to keep his identity somewhat hidden until other aspects of his mission would became clear.

Like Peter, we all hate to suffer or to see others suffer. That's perfectly normal. Our gospel today reveals that the God we worship is a God who takes pity on us in our weaknesses and sufferings and seeks to help us and heal us. I have read and heard of people with healing powers and I personally experienced healings through prayer, especially through the sacrament of the sick. I do not know why God heals some and not others. I do know this: Most often when people ask God for a special favor, they want it to happen like it did in today's gospel: immediately. That would be nice, but it usually doesn't seem to work that way. Remember when Jesus healed 10 lepers, they were not healed until they were on their way to meet with a priest who could declare whether they were clean or not. What I have seen most of the time is that when people pray for something and it doesn't happen they give up praying too soon. But God's ways are not our ways. On some occasions God may use illness or suffering for a purpose we do not understand. On other occasions, God may intervene directly. On still other occasions, God may work through others, especially health care professionals. Although I've seen prayer bring immediate results, more times than not it works better when we don't give up praying but keep at it. Jesus tells us in his teachings on prayer: Keep on asking, keep on knocking with faith. Amen.

1st Sunday of Lent
February 26, 2012

INTRODUCTION – (Gen. 9:8-15; 1 Peter 3:18-22; Mark 1:12-15) I want to call your attention to the word "covenant" in today's first reading, an important concept that will dominate our first readings every week during Lent this year. Typically "covenants" were quite common centuries ago and they were somewhat similar to what we call a "contract" today. A "covenant" was a serious commitment or promise two parties (be they individuals or nations) made to each other. It defined the relationship and the expectations they had of one another. The word "covenant" is not in common use today except when people speak of the marriage covenant. (We also hear it at the consecration of the wine during Mass.) When God chose to enter into a relationship with his people he made a covenant with them. He promised what he would do for them and told them what he expected of them. Today we hear about the covenant God made with Noah and with all of creation after the great flood. Notice this covenant is unusual in that God promises what he will do for his people while he asks nothing of his people in return. St. Peter, in the second reading, tells us the covenant God made with Noah and his family prefigured baptism which is God's pledge to us of salvation and eternal life.

HOMILY – St. Mark begins his gospel by telling us about John the Baptist and his mission of calling people to repent and to prepare for the imminent Day of the Lord. Jesus was baptized by John as a sign that Jesus accepted John's mission and message. After introducing John to us, Mark tells us Jesus was baptized by John. On that occasion the Holy Spirit visibly came down upon Jesus. Mark then tells us immediately the Spirit drove Jesus (the Greek uses a very forceful term here) out into the wilderness. Matthew and Luke tell us of three of the temptations Jesus experienced. Mark, the earliest and shortest of our gospels, tells us simply Jesus was in the wilderness for 40 days, tempted by Satan. I wish to mention just two practical ideas in today's short gospel: 1) no matter how filled with the Spirit we may be, we are not immune from the temptations of the evil one. And 2) sometimes as a person seeks to grow spiritually, there are dry periods, periods when a person feels as if God has abandoned them. Spiritual writers refer to this as a desert period in our spiritual journey. It is a challenge to a person's faith, and yet it is a time of great spiritual growth as a person continues to struggle through it. Numerous saints have described the desert experiences they have gone through. There is a wonderful book by Thomas Green, S.J. called *When the Well Runs Dry* which beautifully describes these periods of dryness and helps a person hold on to their faith through such times. As the Church calls us to use this holy time of Lent to remove some of the distractions that clutter our lives and to focus more on Jesus and on our faith, the Church presents us with the scene of Jesus going off to the wilderness for 40 days to reflect and pray.

Today I have a second topic I would like to touch on. You may have seen in Parish Council minutes or heard rumblings that we have been thinking about cleaning the church for our 150th anniversary next year. I do not believe there is another church in Cincinnati that is more beautiful than St. Boniface. Visitors who come here for the first time always remark how impressed they are with seeing it. We have made some big (and expensive improvements) in past years. Parishioners have always given us support because they love St. Boniface. We continue to make improvements, little ones and big ones. For example we finished St. Patrick's statue, which is back on its stand. We are refurbishing the restrooms. As we often have funeral visitation here in church and there isn't enough room for people to gather, we hope to remove about five pews from the back of church to make a gathering space. Our maintenance men are doing those little projects. The big project that is coming up is painting the church. We wanted simply to clean it, and patch up and touch up bad spots, but we decided there was so much that needed special attention, from the ceiling on down, it made sense to repaint everything. The sanctuary, especially the gold dome, is really filthy. You can see the beams showing up through the paint in the ceiling, and there is more water damage than you would imagine. It's been 50 years since the church has been painted, so it is an opportune time to do so – especially since scaffolding would have had to be put up anyway to do any cleaning and fixing up. We are not going to change the colors. We thought the color scheme is very nice and it has held up very well. We are not going to get rid of the angels in the sanctuary, just clean them up and repair any of them that are damaged. We discovered too, that before we do any repairs or painting, we need a new roof over the two transepts and the sacristies. Otherwise we will very quickly get water damage on our new paint job. Our maintenance man, Al Murnan, has done an excellent job taking care of the roof, but the situation is there are three roofs on top of the two transepts and you cannot find where all the leaks are because they are hidden under other roofs. The insulation between the roofs constantly remains soaked because the water can't evaporate. So getting new roofs comes first. The roof is going to be about $60,000. We recently received a generous donation of $40,000 that will help with the roof. The painting and repair inside church will be about $175,000. I know you are all getting your wallets out in order to make a big donation, but this is not a money talk. What money we need for these projects will come from our reserved funds, but if anyone wants to give any additional help with this we wouldn't turn it down. It should not affect our normal operating expenses as I think that the increased offertory support program we had last fall is doing well. After the last three years when we were in the red, I expect we will come out in the black this year. We may even end up a little ahead which will help us with these projects. I know people like to know what's going on at our parish, so I'm telling you this because I want everyone to know what we are doing to care for our church. I hope to stay here with you as long as I am healthy enough to keep serving. I want to thank everyone for the support they give to St. Boniface. So thank you.

2nd Sunday of Lent
March 4, 2012

INTRODUCTION – (Gen 22:1-2, 9-13, 15-18; Rom 8:31-34; Mark 9:2-10) Last week we heard about God's covenant with Noah; God promised he would never again cause a flood that would destroy all life on earth. The sign of that covenant is the rainbow. Sometime roughly 1750 years before Christ, although the date cannot be established precisely, God entered into another important covenant with a person named Abram. God promised Abram numerous blessings, including many descendants. In return, God asked Abram simply to trust him. Today we hear how Abram (whose name has by now been changed to Abraham) remained trusting in a most difficult situation. Abraham must have felt great anguish when he sensed God was asking him to sacrifice his beloved son, Isaac. Be sure to notice our stained glass window that is above our cry room door. It is a story that reflects great trust on the part of Abraham. I often wonder if God really asked this of Abraham or if Abraham imagined God was asking this of him. Human sacrifice was common to Abraham's culture. At the end of the story, we hear God say, "I swear by myself, that because you acted as you did in not withholding from me your beloved son" then God repeats the blessings he had originally promised Abraham when he saw that Abraham had lived up to his part of the covenant.

HOMILY – As I was reflecting on today's gospel of the Transfiguration, the one feature of the story that struck me was that Jesus took Peter, James and John with him. The rest of the apostles were down at the base of the high mountain trying unsuccessfully to cast out a demon. Jesus was especially close to Peter, James and John. He took them with him when he brought Jairus' daughter back to life. After the Last Supper, when he went to the garden of Gethsemane to pray, all his apostles joined with him, but he invited Peter, James and John to be especially near him. So, as he went up Mt. Tabor, the mountain traditionally identified as the mount of the Transfiguration, only Peter, James and John went with him. Did he need their support and companionship at this particular time?

Many times he prayed alone. He even taught us that when we pray, we should not be like hypocrites who are showy about it, but we should go into our room and shut the door and pray to the Father in secret. (Mt. 6:6) On the other hand, Jesus emphasized the value of not praying alone. He said: "I tell you truly, if two of you agree on earth about anything you ask, it will be done for you by my Father in heaven. For where two or three are gathered in my name, I am there among them." (Mt. 18:19-20) Jesus himself prayed publicly and with others. Often in the gospels we find him in synagogues or in the Temple. All the apostles were with him at the Last Supper when he prayed in their company and he prayed a very lengthy prayer. The whole 17th chapter of John's gospel is called Jesus' high priestly prayer at the Last Supper. Jesus only told us to pray in secret to make the point that we should not be showy about it like some of the Pharisees.

The greatest prayer we have is the Eucharist, when Jesus blessed bread and wine at the Last Supper and changed it into his body and blood. And he told us "Do this in memory of me." How could we ever do what he told us to do if we didn't come together in prayer. The reason this is the greatest prayer we have is because it is a renewal of Jesus' perfect sacrifice on the cross. Jesus is our high priest who at Mass offers his love and obedience to the Father in one perfect act and we are allowed to join in his perfect sacrifice.

In brief, Jesus showed us and taught us that we should pray both in the privacy of our own hearts and that we should pray with one another. What a powerful experience it must have been to be in the company of Jesus when he was praying. Certainly it was a powerful experience for Peter, James and John on this one occasion when Jesus was transfigured on the mountain. If Peter, James and John had not been with him, they would have missed out on this fantastic experience of seeing Jesus in glory. I mentioned earlier that the other apostles were busy at the bottom of the mountain trying to cast out an evil spirit, but they were not having any success. It wasn't until Jesus came down and commanded the spirit to leave that the possessed child was set free from the evil power that controlled him. The apostles asked Jesus why they had no success casting it out and he said, "this kind can only come out through prayer (some manuscripts add 'and fasting')." Jesus had been praying and his prayer was powerful. Peter, James and John, because they were with him, witnessed it all.

I felt this aspect of the Transfiguration needed to be stressed because I feel a lot of people have given up communal prayer. Many say they pray on their own. This is good, but Jesus has shown us, by his example and teaching, the value of praying with others. I heard it said the other day that the second largest Christian denomination in the United States is inactive Catholics. Those who think they don't need to go to "Church" to serve and worship God should know that the word

"Church" in Greek means "a gathering" or "an assembly." How can someone say I belong to this gathering but I don't really belong. The Church teaches that we have a serious obligation as Catholic Christians to come together with Jesus on the Lord's Day to pray together, to offer together to the Father the perfect sacrifice that Jesus gave us at the Last Supper. People sometimes say, "I don't get anything out of it." The question could be asked, "do we pray only to get something? Don't we also pray in order to give something – to give God ourselves, our worship, our love." When we seek to give something is often when we get something. I would suspect that Peter, James and John prayed with Jesus many other times, but this one time, something powerful happened. If they hadn't been with him, they would never have had the experience. St. Francis tells us: "It is in giving that we receive." So let us give thanks to the Lord our God.

3rd Sunday of Lent
March 11, 2012

INTRODUCTION – (Exodus 20: 1-17; 1 Cor. 1:22-25; John 2:13-25) Covenant is a theme that keeps recurring in our first reading these Sundays of Lent. The first Sunday of Lent we hear about God's covenant with Noah. Last Sunday we heard about God's covenant with Abraham and how Abraham's trust in God was tested when he heard God tell him to sacrifice his son. Today, the third Sunday of Lent, we hear about God's covenant with his people as they traveled under the leadership of Moses from slavery in Egypt to the Promised Land. Typically a covenant had two parts, what each party to the covenant promised they would do for one another. God, for his part of the covenant, had promised his people liberty, land, prosperity and his special care and love. Today's first reading tells us what God expected of his people in return for the blessings he promised them.

HOMILY – All four gospels tell us about Jesus cleansing the Temple. John's account of the cleansing of the Temple is at the beginning of Jesus' public ministry, whereas in the other three gospels it occurred shortly before Jesus was put to death. While scholars do not dispute its historicity, they argue about whether it occurred at the beginning or the end of Jesus' ministry. Jesus' zeal for God's house moved him so deeply that he challenged the Temple authorities in the dramatic way we just heard. The money changers and those who sold animals for sacrifice were offering a legitimate service to those who came to offer sacrifice to God, but those changing money from Greek coins to approved Temple currency and those selling the animals for sacrifice obviously took advantage of the people who came to worship. Jesus said that they had made the Temple into a den of thieves. Josephus, the Jewish historian, is quoted as saying that the High Priest, who no doubt benefitted from all these dealings, was "the great procurer of money."

Some scholars see this event more as a sign that the Temple would be destroyed rather than as a cleansing or reform of the Temple practice. The story of this Temple is tragic. It had been under construction for 46 years and it would be roughly another 40 years before it was completed. Then just about 4 or 5 years after completion the Romans destroyed it in the Jewish revolt. Jesus did predict the destruction of the Temple and, even in today's reading, he talks about it being destroyed but he would raise it up in three days. It wasn't until after Jesus' resurrection that his Apostles understood what he was telling them. It was a way for him to say he would replace the Temple and that his sacrifice, because his sacrifice would be a perfect sacrifice, would replace all other sacrifices. We are privileged to be part of that perfect sacrifice of Jesus every time we come to Mass.

Religion has a legitimate need for money. There are buildings to be maintained. There are those dedicated to the service of God who need to have food and clothing and a place to live. The poor need to be helped. Jesus paid the Temple tax. He encouraged people to help the poor. He respected the Temple. Religious people who support the work of religion do not need to be gouged or cheated or taken advantage of. Apparently that's what the Temple authorities were doing and Jesus set them straight.

I know that most of you received a letter from the Archbishop this week asking your help with many of the ministries that take place in our Archdiocese. I hope you read the letter and gave it serious consideration. We have many special collections throughout the year, but this is the really big one (the Catholic Ministries Appeal). You've heard me talk about finances a number of times recently. I don't want you to think I'm doing it because I enjoy it. I would much rather talk about Jesus, but it's my job to occasionally address such practical matters. I want you to know that if I encourage your support of some project, I myself put my money where my mouth is. I don't just talk about it; I support it too.

To be brief, I want to mention just three of the major efforts that the Catholic Ministries Appeal supports: 1) the education of priests, deacons and lay pastoral ministers at the Athenaeum, and if we get more vocations which the Archbishop is trying to do, support for the Athenaeum will be greatly needed; I received my education at the Athenaeum, so did Deacon Ted and

Deacon Jerry, so did our parishioners who went through the Lay Pastoral Ministry Program and who serve or have served our parish so professionally. 2) the collection helps Catholic Charities and Catholic Social Services which provides many services such as counseling, and it offers a number of basic needs to the poor, and 3) it supports retired diocesan priests. We have no pension. This collection for the Catholic Ministries Appeal takes the place of a pension. This collection helps support priests like Fr. Stricker, Fr. Lammeier and about 75 other priests. The demand in this area keeps increasing because priests, like the rest of society, are living longer. I guess if after I retire (if I ever do) and I have to go dumpster diving for my dinner, I didn't do a very good job with my talk on the Catholic Ministries Appeal.

Just those few areas of need I have mentioned take 80 percent of your donation. The other 20 percent will go for chaplains for hospitals and prisons, and St. Rita's School for the Deaf. Nothing is used for Archdiocesan administration. All these worthwhile causes are ministries that are beyond the capability of any single parish, or any group of parishes, to maintain. All parishes need to do their share for the good of the diocese. We will need a few heavy hitters to meet our goal which sets the bar higher than last year. I am proud of St. Boniface. Our parish has met our goal every year for the past 20 years that I've been here. So I am very hopeful we will do it again. Our parish goal is $17,855. The goal is set for each parish based on that parish's Sunday collection. Our collections are better, so our goal is higher. I am going to suggest that if everyone who could afford it, would pledge or donate $100, even if you gave it over a 10 month period, we would make our goal. As I said, we will need a few significant donations to compensate for those who can't donate very much. I hope everyone will pledge or give something, even if it's $5 or $10. In Archbishop Schnurr's letter, there is a pledge card and donation envelope with it. You may send it in to the Archdiocese or to St. Boniface or save yourself 44 cents and bring it with you to church and put it in the collection basket. These many services in our Archdiocese and to the poor in our neighborhoods deserve whatever support we can give. Thank you for your patient listening.

4th Sunday of Lent
March 26, 2006

INTRODUCTION – (2 Chronicles 36:14-16, 19-23; Eph. 2:4-10; John 3:14-21) Our first reading last Sunday was about the covenant God made with his people as they were traveling through the desert on their way from Egypt to the Promised Land. In that covenant God promised his people liberty, land, prosperity and he promised them they would be his special people. What God demanded of his people in return was obedience to his commandments, especially the ones we call "The Ten Commandments." Our first reading this week skips over seven centuries, centuries marked with religious fervor at times, but mostly characterized by indifference to God and to his laws. This indifference took its toll on their strength as a nation and when the powerful Babylonians came against God's people around 600 B.C. they were unable to defend themselves. As a result their land was destroyed and those who managed to survive the Babylonian invasion were enslaved and deported to Babylon. Today's first reading describes this calamity and how God freed them from their Babylonian captivity almost two generations later. Their liberation from

Babylon took place when the Persian king, Cyrus, conquered the Babylonians. Just to help you visualize this, Persia was the land now occupied by Iran and Babylonia was in modern day Iraq. One last thought: next week we will hear Jeremiah promise that God would make a new covenant with his people since the old one was so poorly kept. We celebrate and renew God's new covenant as always as we celebrate the Eucharist today.

HOMILY – One of the central elements of our relationship with God is the idea of covenant. The word "covenant" is not a word we use everyday. It is a solemn and serious agreement, but it is more that that. It is a committed relationship between two people or two groups of people. About the only time we hear the word "covenant" today is in relation to marriage. But in the Bible we hear the word a lot. Last Sunday, this Sunday and next Sunday, in our first reading, we hear passages that referred to the covenant God made with his people. The author of the first reading tells us this covenant was broken more often than it was observed. Instead of giving up on us, however, God offered us a new covenant, sealed in the blood of his Son. It's a covenant we renew and God renews with us every time we come to Mass. God offers this new covenant to all people. As Jesus said: "God gave his only Son so that everyone who believes in him might not perish, but might have eternal life." But not all people want to enter into a covenant of love with this God who sent his son. Again he tells us: "The light came into the world, but people preferred the darkness to light…"

God is our creator who knows us better than we know ourselves. He knows what is for our good, he knows what will lead us to peace and life, eternal life, but he also gave us a free will. He gave us a free will so we would be capable of returning his love. Only a free person can love. But with our free will we can also choose not to love. And making that choice not to love our God points us in a direction that leads away from eternal life and eternal happiness.

People with a concept of "covenant" (even if they've never heard the word "covenant," but who know they are in a relationship of love with God) know a God whom we can call Father, lover, spouse, friend, protector or savior. Without a notion of "covenant" we cannot really know God in a personal way. Without a notion of "covenant" God is seen perhaps as indifferent, overly punitive or overly permissive. I think most people today, who have no notion of "covenant," see God as some kind of indulgent parent who doesn't know how to say "no" and who is so soft hearted he's going to get everyone into heaven no matter how evil they may have been. Jesus did say "God did not send his son into the world to condemn the world," but he also said that whoever does not believe in him is already condemned because they preferred darkness to light. Jesus has done all that is possible, even to the extent of dying for us, so that we can discover the light, the life, the joy that his love can bring, but he cannot force it on us if we are closed to it.

I want to say something about baptism because that's when we begin to live a new life, when we receive the light of Christ, when we enter into a covenant relationship with God. Often I have asked people when they come for the baptism of their child why they want their child baptized. The most common answer is because it washes away original sin. Those who have a deeper understanding of baptism tell me it is because baptism gives their child a sharing in Christ's life. But even that answer is incomplete. Let me draw a comparison between baptism and natural birth. When a child is born, we say they are given the gift of life (although they had already received that gift at conception). But we also know that there's a lot more to being born than simply receiving the gift of life. Natural birth is the beginning of a lengthy, complex process of growth, development, learning and maturation. So too is baptism the beginning of a process of growing in God's love, learning to recognize God as our Father, learning to obey him, worship him, love him, pray to him. That describes a loving relationship with our God that is meant to continue into eternity. One word for that relationship is "covenant." When we come to Mass each week, we come so we don't forget our covenant, that we are sharers in God's life; so we don't forget what Christ has done for us and what he asks of us in this relationship of love. We all know and God knows too how easily we forget things, so he gave us a way to remember: "Do this in memory of me." Thank you for being here today to hear once more of God's love and to express your own love in prayer and praise. Amen.

5th Sunday of Lent
March 25, 2012

INTRODUCTION – (Jeremiah 31:31-35; Hebrews 5:7-9; John 12:20-33) The prophet Jeremiah lived 600 years before Christ. He was sent by God to mercifully warn God's people that they were living on the edge of catastrophe. If they didn't start following God's ways, the Babylonians would invade their land and destroy them. Centuries of wanton idolatry and social injustice had seriously demoralized and weakened God's people. If they followed what God was telling them through Jeremiah, they could avoid disaster. Of course, they ignored Jeremiah and punished him for his message. Today's first reading comes shortly before the Babylonian invasion. God speaks, through Jeremiah, that he is gravely disappointed with the way God's people continually violated the covenant they made with God at Mt. Sinai, a covenant Moses solemnly sealed in blood centuries earlier. In spite of their unfaithfulness, God still loved his people and would make a new covenant with them. Six hundred years later, Jesus used these words "new covenant" when he gave the cup of his blood to his disciples at the Last Supper. We renew that covenant with him each time we come to Mass.

HOMILY – Today's gospel is from John chapter 12, verses 20 to 33. If you would look at verse 1 of this chapter, John tells us it was six days before Passover and Jesus had just arrived in Bethany. Bethany is a little town located on the Mount of Olives just across the Kidron valley from Jerusalem. Just as thousands of other Jews were doing, Jesus was going there to celebrate Passover that year. That year Passover began on Friday evening, so six days before meant Jesus arrived in Bethany sometime on Saturday. Some of his friends, including Martha, Mary, and Lazarus, prepared a dinner for him – not necessarily at their home. It would have to have been a big dinner – remember Jesus had 12 apostles with him. Lazarus, some time before as you know, had been raised from the dead by Jesus, an event that led many Jews to believe in Jesus. While at this dinner, Mary anointed Jesus' feet with expensive perfume. Judas registered a complaint that the gesture was wasteful and the perfume should have been sold so the proceeds could have been given to the poor. Judas, John tells us, was the treasurer for the group. He didn't care for the poor but would steal from the money with which he had been entrusted. Jesus told Judas to "leave her alone. She did it in preparation for my burial." Indeed, Jesus would be buried before the week was over.

John tells us that the next day, which would have been the first day of the week, news got around that Jesus was going into Jerusalem just a couple of miles from where he was in Bethany. When a crowd heard he was going into the city, they met him with palm branches singing "Hosanna. Blessed is he who comes in the name of the Lord." The Pharisees remarked to each other: "We cannot win! Look the whole world has gone after him." Although we won't commemorate Palm Sunday until next week, I wanted to mention this because the anointing at Bethany and the triumphal entry into Jerusalem immediately preceded today's gospel and are connected with it, especially the theme of Jesus' death. After the Pharisees commented that the whole world has gone after him, John tells us it's true. Some Greeks showed up wanting to see Jesus and that's where today's gospel begins.

Most scripture scholars believe that it was after Jesus entered Jerusalem on this occasion that he drove the merchants and money-changers out of the Temple. That's where Matthew, Mark and Luke place the cleansing of the temple in their gospels. But John had already told us about that incident earlier in his gospel, so he does not mention it here. Instead, when these Greek worshippers sought to see Jesus, Jesus saw this as a sign that his hour had come. "Hour" is a key word in John. It described the time he would complete his mission here on earth. It was the time when he would be put to death for faithfully fulfilling his work of teaching, healing, forgiving sins and spreading God's love. It was the time when Jesus would be raised up, both on the cross and in the resurrection, a time when God would manifest to the utmost his presence in his Son.

Today's gospel is Jesus' own reflection on his death. Being human it is not something he wants to go through. "I am troubled now," he says. The Greek word used here does not mean something like a mother telling her children "I am troubled when you don't come when I call you." The Greek word means to experience inward turmoil, to be stirred up, disturbed, unsettled, thrown into confusion. He wonders aloud if he should say: "Father, save me from this hour." If he escaped or ran away, he would abandon all that he had done and all he came to do and his good works would be forgotten forever. He had to face this hour so that he could be glorified and God would be glorified in him. Here the word "glory" does not mean Jesus was looking for human praise. "Glory" in the scriptures means a special revelation of God's presence. It means that he would save us through his death, resurrection and ascension. Jesus gave us an example to help us understand how his death would lead to our salvation. Like a seed must die in order to produce a new growth, so through Jesus' death, resurrection and return to the Father new life would come forth in those who have followed him. He tells us, "where I am, there also will my servant be." We will all face death, but following him involves another kind of death, death to selfishness and sin, and maybe even martyrdom. But death to ourselves will lead to life eternal. As Jesus prays for the strength to get through the ordeal ahead and thus give glory to the Father by fulfilling his mission, God the Father's voice is heard.

The Father's words give testimony about Jesus. The gospel ends on a note of hope for this will be a time of judgment for the world. This means it will look as if evil has won with Jesus' death. But Christ's glorification will put an end to the power of evil in this world.

(Incidentally I read once this is the idea behind April fools day: it's association with Easter. When Jesus rose, the devil, who thought he got rid of Jesus, was made to look a fool.) Evil will not triumph. Jesus will win in the end. We need to keep this optimism in trying times and know that in Jesus is our hope and our life. Amen.

Passion Sunday
April 1, 2012

INTRODUCTION – (Isaiah 50:4-7; Phil 2:6-11; Mark 14:1-15:47) Five hundred years before Christ, a person was described in the Book of Isaiah as God's Servant. The Servant was not identified by name, only by the way the Servant faithfully followed God's call, a call to bring justice to the earth and light to the nations, a call that would result in sacrifice and suffering for the people he came to help. These Servant passages (there are four of them, sometimes called Servant Songs) marvelously describe Jesus. Today's first reading is the first part of the third Servant Song. The first reading is followed by Psalm 22, a meditation on the sufferings of a just person. The first line of this Psalm Jesus prayed as he hung on the cross.

HOMILY – The Missal instructs us that today the homily should be brief. If there any moment of earthly glory for Jesus, his triumphal entry into Jerusalem with people spreading garments and branches in his path was that moment of glory. The people called to him Hosanna (which means "save us") and they recognized that he was coming as Son of David to establish the reign of God. Jesus knew their enthusiasm would be short-lived. He said in John (3:19) "the light has come into the world, and people loved darkness rather than light." Three times he predicted his suffering and death. Even though people can turn away from his light, his light can never be extinguished. It continues to shine for those who welcome it.

He entered Jerusalem in humility and poverty. He is a king who has not come to gain victory by force. He only knocks, and waits for us to open the door. Then he will change our lives, helping us to walk the path he walked, a humble path that leads to the death of our own selfish desires and to our loving others with a sacrificial love like his own.

Like Jesus, we will not very often hear the cheers of the crowd as we make our journey toward eternal life. Mostly our lives will be defined by prayer and obedience to God and by small acts of love for one another. We ask his help to be with us as we make our journey to be with him. Amen.

(I borrowed greatly from *A Devotional Commentary on Mark* by Leo Zanchettin)

Holy Thursday
April 9, 2009

HOMILY – (Exodus 12:1-8, 11-14; 1 Cor 11:23-26; John 13:1-15) Fran told me two weeks ago this is the time of the year when people hang up on her when she calls. That's because for years Fran has been so kind as to recruit people for the foot washing. A lot of people avoid talking to her as we get closer to Holy Thursday. People react like Peter: "Fr. Joe will never wash my feet." Well, I'll admit it is humbling to have your pastor kneel in front of you and wash your feet. For me, though, it's not very humbling at all. I think it's very special. But in Jesus' day it was a different story. It was a dirty job.

People in those days didn't wear shoes and socks. They wore something more like sandals, and most people walked when they went anywhere. They walked the same dusty, dirty roads that herds of animals walked on. So you can imagine people's feet were dirty and smelly. Having their feet washed when they went to someone's house for dinner would have been refreshing. But the master of the house didn't do the foot washing. Slaves or servants did that job and where there were no slaves or servants, the children or the wife did it. I suppose if I wanted to be really humble, I would go wash the feet of several homeless people and have no audience or pretty singing while I was doing it. But we do it tonight to dramatize what Jesus did.

One of our candidates for foot washing remarked, "I don't know what to think about this." Well, Jesus did a lot of teaching and a lot of healing and helping people. But this last night with his apostles before his death, he wanted to really do something off the wall that would stick with them and symbolize what he was all about. So he told them how to think about what he had done. He said: "I have given you a model to follow, so that as I have done for you, you should also do." He had previously told us, "Whoever wishes to be great among you must be your servant, and whoever wishes to be first among you must be your slave." He gave us an example of the great commandment of love; that we should love one another as he has loved us.

But there was an interesting interchange between Jesus and Peter. When Jesus came to Peter, Peter basically asked, "why are you going to wash my feet?" Jesus said, "you don't understand now why I'm doing it, you will understand later." Peter protested, "you will never wash my feet." Jesus said (and I like this translation better), "If I do not wash you, you won't belong to me." That is as strong a statement as Jesus could have made. I asked myself why Jesus was so definite and why it was so important that everyone have their feet washed, even Peter? Thinking of what Jesus was doing as a demonstration of service, it struck me that we all need to allow ourselves to let Jesus serve us. In what ways does he serve us? He serves us through his sacrificial death on the cross and his resurrection. In his words, he came to seek out and to save the one who is lost; and that's all of us. It's only when we know we need to be saved that we will really know Jesus for that's what the name "Jesus" means: God saves. How do we make this connection with his saving love? Two ways: prayer and the sacraments. In those two ways Jesus can serve us and save us.

Especially in the Eucharist does Jesus come to us to bring us the love and life he wants to share with us. He makes himself vulnerable to us. We can receive him with love, we can receive him with indifference, we can receive him with distraction, we can be too busy to bother coming to receive him at all. But for those who open the door of their heart to him, he is there to share a meal with us as friends. (Rev. 3:20) What greater gift can he give us than himself. "My flesh is real food and my blood real drink," he tells us in John's sixth chapter on the Eucharist.

Tonight we recall Jesus' last supper with his disciples. He came to serve them and he did serve them as their teacher and Lord, but now he was about to serve them (and all of us) by his death on a cross. He demonstrated to us how we are to serve one another and gave us a command to do so. And at the Last Supper he gave us a way to remember what he has done for us and how he continues to bring us into union with his saving work, the Eucharist. "Do this in memory of me" we hear him say twice in tonight's second reading, the oldest recorded account of the institution of the Eucharist.

We may not understand it all, we may not understand why Jesus had to die to save us, we may not understand how a small host and a sip of wine can bring Jesus to us, we may not even understand why God would love us so much as to send his Son to save us, but as Jesus said to Peter: "you will understand later." Amen.

Good Friday
April 6, 2012

HOMILY – (Is 52:13-53:12; Heb 4:14-16, 5:7-9; John 18:1-19:42) "We thought of him as stricken, as one smitten by God and afflicted. But he was pierced for our offenses, crushed for our sins; upon him was the chastisement that makes us whole, by his stripes we were healed."

These words of the prophet were written 500 years before Christ. They describe God's Servant who suffered, not for his own sins, but for those of others. This was a difficult concept for God's people to grasp back at that time. According to their theology, if a person was a good person, God rewarded them and if a person was a bad person, God punished them. Since they had no real understanding of heaven and hell at that time in history, they had to conclude that reward and punishment would come about in this life. Thus, the Servant we heard about in today's first reading, who was stricken and afflicted, was thought of as suffering for something evil he, the Servant (whoever it was) must have done. Thus the verse I quoted said: "We thought of him as stricken, as one smitten by God and afflicted" (as though he had been evil).

Another facet of their theology and a major part of their religious practice was offering sacrifices to God. Their sacrifice would be a lamb or an ox or usually another kind of food. The sacrifice they offered was meant to symbolize the gift of themselves to God – a gift they offered to give worship to God, or to ask for a special favor or to seek God's forgiveness for their sins. This made sense to them, that they could offer a sacrifice for something bad they had done hoping God would forgive them. The passage about the Servant introduces a new idea, the idea that someone could offer a sacrifice for the sins of another and make reparation for the evil someone else had done. This was hard for them to understand (hard for us to understand) that the Servant "was pierced for our offenses, crushed for our sins." The Servant's suffering was really serving as a sacrifice before God, and it would bring down God's blessings on his people.

This is a conclusion St. Paul came to about Jesus. Paul was initially a persecutor of those who accepted Jesus as their Savior and Messiah. He was involved in the killing of Stephan the first martyr. He persecuted the Church of God beyond measure and tried to destroy it. (Gal. 1:13) It was considered blasphemy that proclaimed faith in Jesus as Savior and Messiah. Jesus was, after all, a condemned criminal. The Book of Deuteronomy says, "God's curse rests on him who hangs upon a tree." (Deut 21:23) Thus the Jews believed that if God's curse was on Jesus, how could he be considered their Savior and Messiah. But Paul discovered that Jesus became a "curse for us," (Gal. 3:13) and this is how he made that discovery. The risen Jesus appeared to him. It became obvious to Paul that Jesus was not a dead criminal but one uniquely blessed by God. If God had showed him such a unique favor, Jesus must have pleased God in a most unique way. God is not in the habit of bringing people back to life. Jesus did bring a few people back to life, but it was back to the life they had had before. But the risen Jesus enjoyed a life of glory. The Acts of the Apostles describe a Jesus who appeared to Paul in a brilliant light, brighter than the sun in midday. (Acts 26:13) Paul seems to have recognized that Jesus' death could not have been God's curse upon Jesus; it could not have been an accident; it could not have been a punishment for something evil; it had to have been a special blessing from God. It could only have resulted from Jesus' special obedience and love for God. Since, in the Jewish mind death came as the result of sin, Jesus must have borne the curse of death not for anything he had done, but for others. In other words, Jesus' death was a sacrifice for the sins of others. We are freed from our sins if we accept his sacrifice by faith and trust in Christ's death for our salvation. Jesus gave us sacraments, especially Baptism and the Eucharist, to enable us to participate in his saving death. So Paul, the zealous persecutor of the Church, became the zealous defender of the Church and the zealous Apostle and preacher of Jesus as Savior and Messiah. Central to his preaching was the death and resurrection of Jesus. He writes to the Corinthians: "When I came to you proclaiming the mystery of God, I did not come with lofty words or wisdom. For I resolved to know nothing while I was with you except Jesus Christ, and him crucified." (1 Cor. 2:1-2)

This process of viewing Paul's thinking about Jesus' death and resurrection makes sense to me; it has helped me to understand Jesus' death a little better and, hopefully, it will help you too.

Let me end by quoting Isaiah once more: "We thought of him as stricken, as one smitten by God and afflicted. But he was pierced for our offenses, crushed for our sins; upon him was the chastisement that makes us whole, by his stripes we were healed."

(borrowed much from Professor Bart Ehrman in his series of lectures on *The New Testament,* produced by The Teaching Company, Lecture 14)

Easter Vigil & Easter
April 7/8, 2012

HOMILY – A very dedicated parishioner had died and the pastor was sick. Nevertheless, the pastor felt he had to do the funeral services and go to the cemetery, which was 50 miles out of town. To make it easier for the pastor, the funeral director let the pastor ride with him in the front seat of the hearse as they went to the cemetery. After the prayers at the cemetery, the pastor felt even worse and the funeral director suggested that the pastor lie down in the back of the hearse now that the deceased had been buried. On the way home the funeral director stopped to get gas. As the attendant was filling the gas tank, the pastor woke up and peeked out the side window of the hearse. That's when the gas station attendant became a believer in the resurrection. (from *The Joyful Noiseletter,* May-June, 2011, pg 2)

This year most of our gospel readings are from St. Mark. The gospel we just listened to is considered by almost all scholars to be the way St. Mark originally ended his gospel. Although Mark's gospel does tell us about Jesus appearing to the apostles and to many others, it's not something that Mark himself added. Certainly Mark knew about the many appearances of Jesus after the resurrection for Paul tells us about them in his letters, letters that were written 5, 10, 15 years before Mark's gospel was written. Mark ends his gospel by telling us the tomb was empty when some women came looking for Jesus. An angel told the women the reason it was empty was because Jesus had risen. Perhaps in ending this way, Mark wanted us to ask ourselves what the empty tomb means in our lives. Do we believe, as St. Paul tells us, that as Christ was raised from the dead, we too, through our baptism, have come to live in newness of life?

A couple of weeks ago, a friend wrote me a very sad letter. She is divorced, is suffering from physical problems and is depressed. She said "Everyday, everywhere someone is facing a hardship in life." "It's easier to think about a loving God when things are going right. The world is in such a state, how does one stay hopeful?"

Hope grows out of faith. It all depends on what we believe; that is, what we tell ourselves. If we believe that things are hopeless and they will only get worse, then we will be depressed. If we believe that even when things seem hopeless, God will ultimately get us through it all and lead us to a joy that will never end, then we will have hope. This is what Jesus told his apostles at the Last Supper: "You are now in anguish, but I will see you again, and your hearts will rejoice, and no one will take your joy away from you." That's what I tell myself when I'm worried or troubled – that God will make something good come out of this event or this situation. Easter is where we find the faith that brings true and positive hope. We believe that Jesus died and Jesus truly rose from the dead. As St. Paul reminds us, we believe that the destiny of Jesus is also our destiny. We believe that our human body and spirit shares in God's image and likeness. We believe that we, along with all our loved ones who have loved God, will, through the life giving power of God, transformed and live forever. Easter is the "ground-zero" of our faith and the source of all our hope. And so we say, Alleluia (praise the Lord.)

Second Sunday of Easter
April 15, 2012

INTRODUCTION – (Acts 4:32-35; 1 John 5:1-6; John 20:19-31) As most of you know, the Acts of the Apostles was written by Luke, the same Luke that wrote the third gospel. Our first readings, from now until the end of May, will be from the Acts. Luke tells us today about the early Christian community. It must have been very early in the life of the Church because Luke tells us it wasn't long until their system of sharing all things in common began to fall apart. Paul tells us about the problems he had in dealing with the Churches he founded that caused him great anxiety. But for a short time in the beginning, the early Church was of one mind and one heart.

HOMILY – I want to start with a passage from St. Paul's first letter to the Corinthians. Although it is read at Sunday Mass once every three years, I want us to reflect on it now since it is the earliest written account of the resurrection that we possess. Paul writes: "for I handed on to you as of first importance what I also received: that Christ died for our sins in accordance with the scriptures; that he was buried; that he was raised on the third day in accordance with the scriptures; that he was seen by Peter, and then by the Twelve Apostles. After that he was seen by more than five hundred of his followers at one time, most of whom are still living, though some have died by now. Then he was seen by James and later by all the apostles. Last of all, I saw him too, long after the others, as though I had been born at the wrong time." (1 Cor. 15:3-8) Paul wrote this sometime around the year 54, which was before any of the gospels were written. When Paul says, "I handed on to you what I also received" Paul is telling us this has been the Tradition of the Church from the very beginning. Notice Paul refers to some appearances that the gospels do not mention and the gospels mention some that Paul does not. All this week at Mass, and today as well as next Sunday, we hear about Jesus' appearances. Since the apostles were going to be witnesses to the resurrection of Jesus, they had to have seen him alive. They couldn't witness to what they had not seen. Fortified by strength from the Holy Spirit, they were willing to die for what they proclaimed was true. This is the foundation of our faith.

Today's gospel is appropriately timed for this Sunday in that Jesus appeared on Easter Sunday to the apostles and then he appeared again on the following Sunday. Thomas missed out on his first appearance and, being a hard person to convince, he wouldn't believe anyone – the women who saw Jesus Easter morning, the two disciples who saw Jesus Easter Sunday afternoon, and the ten other apostles. (Judas is gone by now you know). So a week later Jesus gave Thomas all the proof he needed. This is the one place in the gospels that tells us Jesus was nailed to the cross, and not just tied to the cross as sometimes happened. Thomas' act of faith, "My Lord and My God," went beyond what Thomas could see with his eyes or touch with his hands. His eyes and his hands gave him proof that Jesus was risen from the dead. Thomas, however, could not see that Jesus was God. It was a pure act of faith for Thomas to declare, "My Lord and my God." Faith is our assent to what we cannot see or touch. Sometimes we can feel God's presence and sometimes we can't, but through faith we always know God is with us and we are one with his Son through grace and the Holy Spirit. Especially we take it on faith that when Jesus said, "This is my body" and "this is the chalice of my blood," the risen Christ is really present to us, even if we cannot see him as the disciples were privileged to do. It is more important to believe in Jesus than to see him – for a lot of people saw Jesus in his lifetime, but they didn't believe. After the resurrection, only those who believed in him saw him; so in our relations with God we can't live by the motto "seeing is believing." The motto we have to live by when it comes to our relationship with God is "believing will lead to seeing." Our believing will bring us to see him for all eternity. So, as Jesus always does, he spoke the truth when he said, " blessed are those who have not seen but have believed."

Recently I heard the story about a man who lost the wife to whom he was married for 70 years and whom he loved deeply. His children were trying to console him, telling him his wife was in a better place (which I'm sure she was – she was a devout believer); they were telling him she was with her parents and her relatives and friends whom she loved; that she was with Jesus. One of their sons, though, told his dad, when you are dead, that is the end of you; there is nothing afterwards. I was horrified by his lack of sensitivity toward his father, trying to deprive his father of any comfort his father might have had through faith in the after life. Furthermore, I thought how would this son know for sure there is nothing? No one knows for sure except someone who has been there. Only Jesus comes from the other side to tell us what's there. The boy who said death is the end is only saying what he chooses to believe, that is what his faith tells him (his belief) – that death is the end of it all. I dare say I could support my faith a lot better than this young boy could support his. Modern psychology had done a lot of study on near-death experiences and this study has shown that there is a lot to look forward to on the other side when our life in this world has come to an end. Most of all, our Christian faith tells us there is life eternal with Jesus and with each other in God. Jesus' resurrection is the preview of what God has planned for all of us who believe in Jesus. Amen.

Third Sunday of Easter
April 22, 2012

INTRODUCTION – (Acts 3:13-15, 17-19; 1 John 2:1-5a; Luke 24:35-48) In our first reading, there is no mention of a crippled man being healed by Peter and John, but this is the context of Peter's speech that we are about to hear from the Acts of the Apostles. A man, lame from birth, was brought to the Temple every day so he could beg for alms. Remember, in the Jewish mentality of the time, this man was not only physically impaired, but everyone would have looked upon him as a very sin-full person. The Jews would have thought that God was punishing him for something he or his parents must have done. A short time after the coming of the Spirit on Pentecost, Peter and John went to the Temple for afternoon prayer. The lame man saw them and asked for a little money. Peter said, "I don't have any money, but I will give you what I have. In the name of Jesus Christ of Nazareth, get up and walk." Then Peter helped him to his feet and he was healed. He was so excited, he jumped and danced and praised God. Of course, this created quite a commotion and everyone wondered what had happed. It was a perfect opportunity for Peter to explain the healing power of the risen Jesus. Notice Peter is very outspoken in accusing all of his Jewish listeners, not just their leaders, of rejecting Jesus and calling for his death. Peter said God can excuse them because they acted out of ignorance, but from now on they have no excuse, and they must repent and be converted for they had just seen the risen Jesus at work in the healing of the lame man. It is not the entire speech of Peter, but it is the most important part of it.

HOMILY – I came across an interesting parable the other day about an old pine tree. It was tall, 70 feet above the forest. Younger trees were also tall but none of them had a top as filled with foliage as the old pine. It was scarred from wind and lightening but it had survived every challenge that came along. Even when strong winds snapped off the younger pines, this old pine barely lost a needle. Amazingly, what finally destroyed this grand old pine tree was not a storm; it was a heavy snow that piled up on its branches. No one would be able to say which snowflake was the proverbial "last straw" that accomplished what years of storms had been unable to do, but the weight of many tiny snowflakes snapped off the old tree's magnificent and full crown.

The article where I read this parable was talking about debt. Most of us know that debt is something that can slowly–but–significantly erode one's economic ability to recover. One little thing can tip the scales from a person's carrying a lot of debt to becoming bankrupt?

However, I thought the parable was equally true of how sin can destroy us. Sin is a reality for all of us. St. John says at the beginning of his letter: "if we say, 'we are without sin,' we deceive ourselves." We confess as we begin each Mass that we are sinners and ask for God's mercy. Like tiny, innocuous looking snowflakes, sin can have a way of creeping up on us. We tell ourselves things like "oh, that's not so bad," or "everybody's doing it," or "God is forgiving," or "no one will know," "nobody's perfect," or whatever. For the most part, each of these statements can be absolutely true: it's not so bad, everybody's doing it, God is forgiving, no one will know, nobody's perfect but like little snowflakes that keep falling, we don't notice how certain habits can grow. St. John tells us in today's second reading "I am writing this to you so that you may not commit sin." Before I move in a more positive direction with what I have to say about sin, I would like to insert what I believe is the most dangerous sin our culture has to deal with today – ignoring the Third Commandment, to keep holy the Lord's Day. To too many people it doesn't seem to be a big deal, yet it denies God the honor due to God and it breaks one's connection with the body of Christ, the community of believers, which gives us spiritual nourishment and guidance.

St. John has more to say about sin than to tell us we're all guilty. He goes on to say, "if anyone does sin, we have an Advocate with the Father, Jesus Christ the righteous one." Our readings at this time of the year proclaim the resurrection, but they also continuously call us to live the new life Christ came to bring us and to turn away from whatever interferes with our relationship with our risen Lord. Did you notice how in last Sunday's gospel, the first thing Jesus said to the apostles after greeting them with "Peace be with you," he said "Receive the Holy Spirit, whose sins you forgive they are forgiven them"? In our first reading, Peter calls his listeners to repent and be converted that their sins may be wiped away. In today's gospel, Jesus tells his apostles, "Thus it is written that the Christ would suffer and rise from the dead on the third day and that repentance, for the forgiveness of sins, would be preached in his name to all the nations."

Dr. Karl Menninger, a well-known psychiatrist, wrote a very perceptive book entitled *Whatever Became of Sin.* He ends his book by saying the first thing we have to do to change anything about ourselves that perhaps we should change is to face it. Last Sunday is often designated as Diving Mercy Sunday. I'm all for Divine Mercy and I'm grateful that God's mercy is available any time we turn to him and ask his forgiveness. I suppose it's called Divine Mercy Sunday because of last week's gospel, but today has every right to be called Divine Mercy Sunday. Truly, on every Sunday, or every time we come to Mass, we begin asking for God's mercy. We say in the Our Father, "forgive us our trespasses;" we say before Communion, "Lord I am not worthy."

I suppose if a person is burdened with guilt, Divine Mercy Sunday would be a good reminder that God is merciful and forgives us when we turn back to him, but we must always know God is kind and merciful. It's the way he identified himself to Moses (Exodus 34:6), the way he identified himself throughout the whole Old Testament, the way he presents himself to us in Jesus, and for that we give thanks.

Fourth Sunday of Easter
April 29, 2012

INTRODUCTION – (Acts 4:8-12; 1 John 3:1-2; John 10:11-18) Last week in my introduction to the first reading from the Acts of the Apostles I spoke about how Peter and John healed a crippled beggar in the Temple. The healed man jumped up and down and was walking around which caused a great amount of commotion in the Temple. Those who were in the Temple at the time wanted to know what happened and how it had happened. Peter's speech on that occasion was the first reading last week. Peter gave all the credit to the risen Jesus who had healed the man through the Apostles. Many of the Jewish religious leaders did not believe in the possibility of a resurrection. When they heard what was going on, they arrested Peter and John. They didn't want to hear any more about Jesus who was a threat to their position. Today we hear a portion of Peter's testimony before the Jewish court. Notice not only what Peter had to say about Jesus but also his boldness. The court didn't know what to do with Peter and John for all the people in Jerusalem were excited and happy about the healing of the man who had been lame for over 40 years. So the court officials warned the Apostles not to talk about Jesus any more. The Apostles were not intimidated for they were now filled with the Holy Spirit. (Acts 4:8-12)

HOMILY – Two ladies from New York had always lived a pretty sheltered life. One day they decided to take a trip to England. While they were touring the countryside, the one said to the other: "Look at those white cows. I've never seen cows like that before." The other replied: "Maybe they are albino. Or perhaps a special British type of cow." The guy sitting behind them said: "Those cows are sheep." Sheep are not as common a sight in the U.S. as they are in other countries – especially in the Middle East. On a trip several years ago, we saw a lot of sheep in Israel. Once or twice our tour bus had to stop for about five minutes or so as a very large flock of sheep crossed the road with their shepherd.

I know I've mentioned this before, but it was one of the most beautiful sights was as I was coming down Mt. Sinai. It took, I think, about eight hours to climb up and as we were coming down we saw a shepherdess with her little flock of sheep scattered on a nearby mountain trying to find bits and pieces of vegetation on the barren rocks. As we watched this peaceful scene as the sun was going down, she got out her shepherds' flute and started walking toward wherever she lived. As she played a little tune, the sheep all fell into line and followed her until they rounded a bend and were out of sight. Jesus says of the shepherd: "he walks ahead of them, and the sheep follow him." (Jn 10:4) Because sheep were a major part of Jewish life, culture and economy, Jesus' listeners could relate to what Jesus preached a lot more easily than we can.

What Jesus said about shepherds we would understand better by making comparisons with dedicated parents or security personnel such as the firemen and policemen and women who sacrificed their lives on 9/11 to save others.

One thing that will help us understand Jesus' parable of the good shepherd is to look back in the Old Testament to the Book of Ezekiel. God condemned the kings and priests at the time of the prophet Ezekiel (almost 600 years before Christ), because they were leading people away from God and not closer to God – which they should have done. Ezekiel compared the

Jewish leaders to shepherds who had no concern for the sheep, the people, but they used the people only to enrich themselves. Ezekiel tells these wicked leaders: "Thus says the Lord God: I myself will look after and tend my sheep. In good pastures will I pasture them. I will give them rest, the lost I will seek out, the strayed I will bring back, the injured I will bind up, the sick I will heal shepherding them rightly." (Ezekiel 34:11)

Jesus is the fulfillment of Ezekiel's prophecy. He continues to guide us to eternal life, if we will follow him. We have all gone through those times when we don't know where he's taking us, perhaps many times. That's why he tells us to trust him.

I am reminded of a little story. A holy man took a trip to a town with which he was unfamiliar. He took with him a lamp, a rooster and a donkey. When he could not find a place to stay in the town, he went into the nearby woods to sleep. He lit his lamp to read the Scriptures, but a strong wind blew the lamp over and it broke. So he said, "all that God does, he does well" and fell asleep. During the night, wild animals chased away the rooster and thieves stole the donkey. When he woke as the sun came up, they were gone, yet the holy man said, "all that God does, he does well." He then went back into the village to see if any rooms where he could stay had become available. When he got there he discovered enemy soldiers had been there during the night and killed everyone in the town. He also learned these enemy soldiers had traveled through the part of the woods where he was sleeping. Had his lamp not been broken, he would have been discovered. Had not the rooster been chased, it would have crowed, giving him away. Had not he donkey been stolen, it would have brayed. So once more the holy man declared: "All that

God does, he does well." We just have to be careful not to say that every bad thing that happens is God's doing. People do bad things against God's wise plan or against God's laws out of ignorance or evil or for whatever reason. We have to remember what Paul said: "for those who love God, everything works out for the best." Amen.

Fifth Sunday of Easter
May 6, 2012

INTRODUCTION – (Acts 9:26-31; 1 John 3:18-24; John 15:1-8) During the Easter season, our first reading is always from the Acts of the Apostles. The Acts of the Apostles tells us how the Risen Christ, through the Holy Spirit, continued to be with his Church and guide his Church and how the Church spread so rapidly. Today's reading begins to tell us about one of those most responsible for the spread of the gospel: St. Paul. Many of the Jews, because they were under Roman occupation, had two names – a Roman name and a Jewish name. Paul's Roman name was Paul and his Jewish name was Saul. Most of the time he is called Paul, but occasionally, as in today's first reading, he is called Saul. You remember he was a zealous Pharisee and a fierce persecutor of all who believed in Christ. He was most likely one of the leaders of the crowd who killed Stephen, the first martyr. On one occasion, as he was on his way to Damascus to search out Christians and arrest them, Jesus appeared to him. In an instant Paul realized Christians had it right and he was 100 percent wrong. His life turned around completely and he began preaching and teaching about Jesus, that he was Savior and Messiah. Even after Paul preached about Jesus for three years, the Christian community in Jerusalem was not convinced that he could be trusted. When he first showed up in Jerusalem, the disciples were afraid of him. Barnabas was a disciple the Jerusalem community did trust and he testified that Paul was genuine. Thus, through Barnabas, Paul was welcomed into the community. However, the Hellenists, a term used to describe Greek speaking Jews, refused to accept Paul and saw him as a traitor to Judaism. For his own safety, Paul had to leave Jerusalem. He headed back to his hometown of Tarsus in modern day Turkey.

HOMILY – Forgive me for this old story. One day the Holy Father decided to visit the sick in a nursing home. He came to the room of one old man who showed no excitement or even any recognition that this was the Holy Father coming to see him. So the Holy Father asked him, "Do you know who I am?" The old man said, "No, but if you ask the nurse at the desk, she will tell you."

Jesus tried to tell us in so many ways who he was. Especially in St. John's gospel, Jesus often uses the words "I am." Sometimes he uses "I am" without a predicate such as when he said "Amen, Amen, I say to you, before Abraham came to be, I am." (Jn. 8:58) Other times Jesus used images to describe himself such as: "I am the light of the world," (Jn. 9:5) or "I am the resurrection and the life," (Jn. 11:25) or "I am the good shepherd," (Jn. 10:11) or "I am the bread of life," (Jn. 6:35) or as we hear today: "I am the vine, you are the branches," (Jn. 15:5).

As I was reflecting on today's gospel, two of these "I am" statements came together in an image that impressed itself on me: "I am the bread of life," and "I am the vine, you are the branches." They came together in this image: picture a grape vine coming from the altar during Mass. It extends itself down the center aisle of church at the same time branching out down the side aisles. It continues to branch out all the way to the back of church to encircle and embrace each person who is here. The divine life and love that is alive in that vine brings divine life and love to each person here. Wherever you are sitting, it reaches out to all. Making each of us part of this vine is a wonderful gift God gives us.

Notice, a vine is not just the stem but the vine is the stem and all the leaves and all the branches and all the fruit. The vine is everything that is alive and growing. Jesus is the vine, and through grace and the Eucharist, we become part of him, and he becomes part of us. We can't live without him any more than a branch that is broken away from its source of life can live on its own. United with him, we live; we live a life we are often not aware of – just like an unborn infant is probably not aware of the life that it is beginning to live. But that life is there. John tells us in his first letter: "beloved, we are God's children now; what we shall be has not yet been revealed. We do know that when it is revealed we shall be like him, for we shall see him as he is." (1 Jn. 3:2) Jesus extends his life and his love to us, which we first received in baptism and which he continues to feed in us through the bread of life.

It is comforting to picture Jesus' life and love reaching out to each of us, but Jesus also reminds us we can't just put it in a box and store it away in a cupboard. It is meant to be dynamic. His life and love are meant to be lived in a life of holiness, a life that flows from his teachings, (not simply What Would Jesus Do, because we can't presume to know what he would do, but what did Jesus teach us we should do). It should be a life of not just thinking of ourselves all the time. Certainly we have to take care of ourselves because if we don't know one else will, but our lives must include consideration for others. Quite simply, this is the fruit God looks for: good works. There's a lot to think about in this one little "I am" statement: "I am the vine, you are the branches." We thank him for that; we pray we will live up to the responsibility it lays on us; and we have the Eucharist to strengthen us and help us. Amen.

Sixth Sunday of Easter
May 13, 2012

INTRODUCTION – (Acts 10:25-26, 34-35, 44-48; 1 Jn: 4:7-10; Jn 15:9-17) As the message of Jesus started to spread, a major issue arose in the early Church. Jesus was a Jew, the Apostles were Jews, and Jesus' first followers were Jews. Jesus had taught people to worship, to love the God of the Jews, and to follow the commandments God gave the Jews. What should Gentiles, who were pagans, do when they became believers and followers of Jesus? Many Jews insisted they should first convert to Judaism before they could accept Jesus as their Savior. They insisted men had to be circumcised and all must follow Jewish dietary laws, Jewish feasts, offer sacrifices in the Temple as prescribed in the Torah. This is the issue that is behind today's first reading. (Acts 10:25-26, 34-35, 44-48)

St. Peter, the leader of the community of those who believed in Jesus, received the answer to this question in a very unusual way. While Peter was in prayer, God gave Peter a vision of many different birds and animals. Many of them were birds and animals the Jews were not allowed to eat, such as pork, shrimp, clams, oysters and many other creatures. (Lev. 11:1-23) God told Peter to eat them. Peter said he would never eat any food that the Law called unclean. God said to him: "What God has made clean, you are not to call unclean." God said this three times to Peter. Then when the vision disappeared, God told Peter there were some men coming to see him and he was to go with them to the home of a Gentile named Cornelius, a high officer in the Roman army. A strict Jew was not allowed to enter a Gentile's house, but God told him to, so Peter did. Cornelius had a gathering of many relatives and friends (all pagan) at his home waiting for Peter. Cornelius told Peter about an angel who had appeared to him and had told him to send for Peter. So Peter spoke to the group about Jesus. Almost Peter's entire speech has been left out of our reading, but you can look it up in your Bibles when you get home. Today's liturgy wants to focus on the response of the pagan Gentiles, how the Holy Spirit came upon them and how Peter baptized them without insisting that they first convert to Judaism before accepting Jesus into their lives.

HOMILY – (2nd Reading: 1 Jn: 4:7-10; Gospel: Jn 15:9-17) Probably most of you saw the Sunday comics last week. There was one especially appropriate for today. In Baby Blues the mother was having a nice relaxing bath when two of her children came banging on the bathroom door screaming, "Mom, Mom." Mom calls, "What?" The kids answer, "we need you." "What's wrong? Is it serious" Mom asks. The kids holler, "Come quick." Mom, with soapy hair and all wet, throws a towel around herself and rushes out of the bathroom, jumping over the toys and clothes and other items tossed around the room, shouting, "I'm coming, I'm coming." By now the kids are in the living room looking out the window, shouting "Hurry, hurry." Mom makes it to the living room panting, "I'm here – what is it – a fire, accident, injury?" They answer, "Ice Cream truck. Thanks to you we missed it. What took you so long?"

Happy Mother's Day! If the mom treated her children with patience and kindness rather than killing them, which she might have felt like doing, she was following the description of love we find in St. Paul's letter to the Corinthians: "love is patient, love is kind, etc." a passage we often hear at weddings.

Today's gospel on love is a perfect gospel for Mother's Day. Surely most of us first learned about love from our parents, but if you grew up in a home like I did, where mother was always there for her children, it was from our mothers that we experienced love all day long.

Love, as we all know, is not just warm fuzzy feelings; it is dedication and commitment; it is care; it is unselfishness and thoughtfulness; it is patience and kindness; it is forgiveness. Warm fuzzy feelings come and go, and that's why Jesus said love is a commandment. We don't always feel like being loving – whether toward God or toward one another. Thus we spend time in prayer at times when we don't feel like praying. Prayer is a way we show our faith and our love for God. We do a favor for someone who needs our help simply because they need our help and it's the loving thing to do. Jesus said to love our neighbor as ourselves, so love presupposes we love ourselves – not in a selfish way but in a healthy way. If we don't love ourselves, how are we going to love our neighbor? In today's gospel, however, Jesus even ups the ante when he says, "love one another as I love you." We can't love like him – in such an unselfish way – without his help, which we all need every day.

Jesus will give us that help if we ask. There are two lines in today's gospel that always impress me. The one line spoke clearly to me when I was a young priest. I was working hard teaching, counseling, visiting the sick and so on, but I was not praying nearly enough. Once when I was praying, I heard our Lord say to me: "I no longer call you slaves I have called you friends." I realized Jesus wanted not only my ministry, but he wanted me to spend a little more quiet time alone with him, talking to him and listening to him. He wants a relationship that is one of friendship and friendship doesn't happen without spending time with our friend .

The other part of the gospel that always speaks to me is Jesus' statement: "I have told you this so that my joy may be in you and your joy might be complete." We all want to be joyful. None of us likes being depressed or miserable. Well, here's one of the ways to joy, love – love of God and love for one another. If you want to be more joyful, pray to be more loving. Amen.

Feast of the Ascension
May 20, 2012

HOMILY – (Acts 1:1-11; Eph 4:1-13; Mark 16:15-20) Jesus promised that those who believe in him would be able to perform many powerful signs: healing the sick, casting out demons, praying in tongues, being bit by serpents without any ill effect and a few others. Probably all of these signs reflect the miraculous powers given to the Apostles in the early Church, including once when St. Paul was bitten by a viper on the Island of Melita (Acts 28:3) and nothing happened to him. That event brought a lot of conversions. The Church to this day still has a sacrament for the sick, still does exorcisms, and some believers pray in tongues. All of the people I know still avoid snakes.

I want to tell you a story. A man who was not a frequent church goer decided to go to church with his wife one Sunday. She went to a very fundamentalist denomination that took every word in the Bible literally.

During the service this gospel was read and after the reading the pastor walked down the main aisle of church, picked up a large box, opened it up and it was filled with all kinds of snakes. He started handing them out to people as he walked up the aisle, asking them to prove their faith. The husband asked his wife, "you don't think he's going to hand me one of those, do you." "I don't know," she said. "Well," he said, looking around the room, "where's the back door?" "There ain't none," she replied. "Well then," the husband asked, "where do you think they would like to have one?" (*The Joyful Noiseletter*, April 2009)

I don't think Jesus expects us to go around testing God by deliberately getting bit by serpents. Jesus expects us to use our good sense. He himself told Satan, "you shall not put the Lord, your God, to the test" when Satan was tempting Jesus to throw himself off the parapet of the Temple.

Our first reading is the beginning of the Acts of the Apostles. It is St. Luke's second volume showing how the work of Jesus continued after his ascension. As he begins the book of Acts, Luke briefly gives us a recapitulation of what he has already told us in his gospel about Jesus' work, his death and his resurrection. We heard Luke tell us in today's first reading that for 40 days Jesus continued to appear to the Apostles and teach them about the kingdom. There is no other mention of 40 days in the Acts of the Apostles, other than the period of time during which Jesus appeared to the Apostles. When we read this passage, it sounds as if Jesus didn't ascend to the Father until after he finished appearing. But Luke tells us in his gospel it was on Easter Sunday night when Jesus ascended. I think he first ascended then started appearing to the Apostles for a period of time until he thought they were sufficiently prepared to do the work he wanted them to do.

The number 40 is a round number meaning something like between 25 and 45. It is a number that is often used symbolically as a time of preparation. Remember God's chosen people spent 40 years in the desert in preparation to enter the promised land, Elijah walked 40 days and 40 nights to Mt. Horeb as he prepared for the next part of his calling, Jesus spent 40 days fasting in the desert before he began his public ministry. Jesus' appearances after the resurrection for 40 days, as presented here in Luke, suggests that Jesus was teaching and preparing his Apostles to go out and continue his work.

Of all the things Jesus and his Apostles may have talked about, Luke draws special attention to a burning issue in the early Church. The Apostles ask Jesus, "Lord, are you at this time going to restore the kingdom to Israel?" They were all thinking apocalyptically; that is, they were looking forward to the time when God would punish their enemies, raise the dead to life and establish his kingdom of peace and justice when the Messiah would rule the world. We see this was a real issue in the early Church in some of the letters of St. Paul. After 2000 years it still hasn't happened. Through the centuries many people have predicted when this would take place. Jesus never gave an answer to that question, and those who have tried to figure it out have always failed. So when people try to predict the end of the world and the second coming of Christ, the odds say they will be wrong. We seldom think much about it but our Lord tells us that we should be concerned so that we are prepared and when the Lord comes he will find us living the way God wants us to.

I have been talking about the first reading from Luke, but before I conclude I should say something about the gospel from Mark. Mark ends his brief description of Jesus' ascension by telling us Jesus is now seated at the right hand of the Father. In effect, Mark is saying that Jesus was at the same level of power and importance as God, above every principality, authority, power, and dominion and every thing that ever existed or will exist as Paul tells us in the second reading. Being seated at God's right hand is one of the earliest ways of expressing Jesus' glorification. Later the Church gave a clearer description of Jesus' position vis-a-vis the Father. In the Council of Nicea, the Church officially defined that Jesus is equal to and of the divine being with the Father. The Council used the word "consubstantial" with the Father, a word that means "of the same substance." We say this in the Creed each week.

In contrast to Mark, Luke, in the Acts of the Apostles, ends his description of the ascension using a somewhat different image. Jesus is hidden from view by a cloud or even raised up by a cloud. In other words, Jesus entered into a world that is beyond what we can know about while we are still in this present life. As Paul said, "eye has not seen, nor ear heard, nor has it entered into people's hearts what God has prepared for those who love him." The great theologian, St. Thomas Aquinas, who clearly and beautifully wrote volumes about God and the life of faith, had a mystical experience while saying Mass. He somehow saw beyond that cloud and experienced the glory of God. After that he stopped writing. People asked why and he said something like: "what I have seen makes all my writing look like straw in comparison." Besides representing the glory of heaven which cannot be seen, a cloud in the Bible is also a symbol of divinity. Remember it was a cloud that led the people of God through the desert as they traveled to the Promised Land. It was a cloud that filled Solomon's Temple when God made it his dwelling place. Through different images, Luke and Mark are telling us that Jesus entered into the fullness of glory that was rightfully his. The Ascension, however, is not just about the glorification of Jesus; it is also a feast of hope for us, for where Christ has gone, he has promised that we who live as he has taught us will certainly follow. It is one of the few guarantees that we can have in this life. Amen.

Seventh Sunday of Easter
May 16, 1999

HOMILY – (Acts 1:15-17, 20-26, 1 John 4:11-16, John 17:11-19) Jesus was asked one time what is the most important commandment in the law. We know how he answered. He not only gave us the most important commandment but the second most important commandment as well, two commands that perfectly compliment each other: to love God with our whole heart and soul and mind and strength and to love our neighbor as ourselves. Jesus gave us the answer not only by his words but also by the way he lived. I would like to reflect today on how Jesus showed love for his Father. His perfect obedience was one way he showed his love. Another way he showed it was by spending time with his Father in prayer. That is what I especially want to focus on today. The topic of prayer was inspired by today's gospel which is part of Jesus prayer at the Last Supper. We have little or no information about what his life was like before he began his public ministry. The little information we do have shows us that Joseph and Mary were faithful in their Jewish observances. Thus Jesus would have been brought up in that tradition, going to synagogue on the Sabbath and going to the

Temple in Jerusalem annually for Passover. St. Luke tells us that when Jesus was beginning his ministry he went to Nazareth and went to the synagogue on the Sabbath "according to his custom." Synagogue services would have been very similar to the first part of our Mass. There would be common prayer and readings from the Law and the prophets and with a commentary after each reading. St. Luke points out in his gospel that Jesus was praying as John the Baptist baptized him. Immediately after that, recall how Jesus went into the desert for 40 days to fast and pray. His encounter with the devil there showed he knew the scriptures well and he could quote them easily.

Frequently it is mentioned that during his public ministry Jesus was at the Temple participating in liturgical celebrations there. The gospels tell us about Jesus getting up early in the morning to pray or staying up all night in prayer. He would spend time in prayer before important decisions or important events. One time after seeing Jesus praying, the disciples asked him to teach them to pray and of course we are all familiar with the prayer he taught them. In addition to the Our Father, Jesus taught a lot about prayer. For example the parable of a man who had a friend visit him at night and he went to his neighbor to borrow some food, and he kept on knocking until he got what he needed. That's the way Jesus said we should pray. Even when he wasn't teaching about prayer, his teachings reflect the deep relationship Jesus had with his Father. There is no doubt about it, prayer played a major role in Jesus life. The Last Supper of course was more than an ordinary supper. It was the Passover which Jesus was celebrating with his disciples, which was a religious celebration.

His prayer (in the 17th chapter of John) is divided into three parts. First Jesus prays for himself, then for his apostles, then for all who would come to believe in him. Notice how many times the word "glory" is used in today's gospel. Jesus saw his death and resurrection as a moment of glory, a moment when God's saving love would be revealed to the world. He prays that the Father might be glorified in all that was to take place and that in the fulfillment of his mission, he might be a source of life for all who would believe in him. It is comforting to know he prayed for all of us at the Last Supper. He continues to intercede for us each time we celebrate the Lord's Supper.

There is not the time to analyze this prayer thoroughly. My main point today was simply to point out the prayerfulness of Jesus. We see in the first reading how Jesus followers imitated his example as they gathered together in prayer in the upper room after the Ascension, waiting for the coming of the Holy Spirit. Louis Evely in his book, *Teach us to Pray*, wrote: "Too many Christians regard God as pilots regard their parachute, namely, good if needed, but better if they can get along without it." We might wonder why would Jesus need to pray? He was already as close to the Father as he possibly could be. I am sure there are many reasons why Jesus prayed, but this question might best be answered with another question: "why do we need to spend time with those who are important to us, with those whom we love?"

A true disciple of our Lord will make prayer a priority in their lives, and by "prayer" I mean more than just a rapidly recited Our Father or Hail Mary. Prayer is spending time with our God. Do we feel like we're too busy? I will never forget what our spiritual director in the seminary told us. The busier we are the more we need to pray.

Today we come together for the greatest prayer there is. As we gather in prayer today, we are not alone and I don't mean simply that there are others here in church with us. Christ is with us and it is in union with his perfect sacrifice of love and obedience on the cross that we offer our prayers and praise to God our Father.

Pentecost
May 27, 2012

INTRODUCTION – (Acts 2:1-11; 1 Cor 12:3b-7, 12-13; John 20:19-23) Our first reading is from the prophet Joel, one of the 12 minor prophets. About the only time we hear from this prophet is on Ash Wednesday. Joel lived during a great plague of locusts who would likely have destroyed all the crops the people depended on for food and there would have been a terrible famine. He called all God's people to a time of serious prayer and fasting. (That's why he is read on Ash Wednesday.) Today's first reading was probably a pronouncement by the prophet after the locusts were gone. Joel sees God at work in rescuing his people from famine and from the plague. As such, God's spirit brings life and salvation for those who call on the name of the Lord. St. Peter uses this passage almost in its entirety to explain that the coming of the Holy Spirit upon Jesus' disciples at Pentecost is the fulfillment of the words of the prophet.

INTRODUCTION – We hear in our first reading St. Luke's account in the Acts of the Apostles of the coming of the Holy Spirit on Pentecost. The Spirit came with a loud noise, tongues of fire, and the gift of the apostles being able to speak new languages. The coming of the Holy Spirit took place in the presence of Jews from all over the world. However, the greatest sign of God's Spirit at work was the courage shown in the apostles, especially Peter who just weeks before denied three times that he even knew Christ.

HOMILY – Pentecost is one of the oldest and one of the three most important feasts of the Jewish people. That's why there were so many people in Jerusalem when the Holy Spirit came down on Jesus' disciples. It is believed to have originally been an agricultural feast. Somewhere in the course of time it began to be celebrated as the anniversary of the giving of the law to Moses on Mt. Sinai. It is because of the coming of the Holy Spirit that Pentecost has also become one of the three most important feasts in our liturgical calendar. I always ask people to wear something red to remind all of us that this is a special day.

Through the outpouring of the Spirit the Church, under the leadership of Peter and the Apostles, received the power and the commission to speak to all nations and to be understood by them. Through the gift of the Spirit, Jesus continues his work of bringing God's life and love to all of us. Almost every book in the New Testament speaks to us about the action of the Spirit guiding the Church and guiding each of us closer to God.

Paul especially tells us the Spirit helps us to believe in Jesus (no one can say Jesus is Lord except by the Holy Spirit). The Spirit helps us to pray, even as we are often plagued with distractions. The Spirit helps us live lives of love, joy, peace, patience, kindness, generosity, faithfulness, gentleness and self-control. The Spirit enlightens us to know God's way and to live it. The Spirit calls us to unity with Christ and with one another, something Jesus desires and earnestly prayed for at the Last Supper. St. Paul tells us, "in one Spirit we were all baptized into one body" The Spirit dwells in us as St. Paul tells the Corinthians who thought they could use their bodies any way they chose. He teaches us that our bodies are temples of the Holy Spirit. (1 Cor. 6:19) Through the Spirit, Christ gives us forgiveness in the Sacrament of Reconciliation for Jesus said to the apostles, "whose sins you forgive they are forgiven them." There is no end to what we could say about the Spirit, for the Spirit is infinite for the Spirit is God.

I would like to share with you some of the ways I have experienced the Spirit at work. Sometimes (and it has happened often) I have been reading the Scriptures and a particular verse seems to jump off the page. I feel it deep inside that God is speaking to me personally through that verse. Or when I am counseling or visiting the sick, something brilliant comes out of my mouth and I realize that idea didn't come from me, it was God's Spirit speaking. When I do something to help someone and I get that really good feeling inside, that's the Holy Spirit at work. I'm sure everyone here has experienced that feeling. Of course, the Spirit is at work in my ministry as a priest, saying Mass, consecrating the bread and wine, forgiving sin, anointing the sick.

We call God's Spirit the Holy Spirit for there are other spirits that are not holy. I believe there are evil spirits; I believe there is a spirit in our world today that does not mirror the Holy Spirit, but is rather a spirit of making up one's own rules in life, independent of what God wants of us. If a person wants to identify themselves as a "spiritual person," they should ask themselves what spirit it is that is directing their lives. If they desire everlasting life and happiness, it is only by the Holy Spirit that they will achieve it.

There is one line in the Scriptures that I love. Jesus

said, "if you who are evil know how to give good gifts to your children, how much more will the heavenly Father give the Holy Spirit to those who ask him?" (Lk. 11:13) Do not hesitate to ask for the Holy Spirit. God will not deny you your request.

Trinity Sunday
June 3, 2012

INTRODUCTION – (Deut 4:32-34, 39-40; Rom 8:14-17; Mt 28:16-20) As far back in history as we know, humans have believed in divine beings whom they considered to be either friendly or hostile to us humans. Forms of worship developed to please those divine beings who were friendly or to protect oneself from those who were unfriendly. Some cultures had hundreds of such divine beings. Can you imagine having to be concerned about each one of these powerful entities without getting on the wrong side of any one of them. Polytheism (the worship of many gods) was practiced everywhere. Abraham and his descendants were an exception to the rule. Abraham may have acknowledged there were many other gods in many other places, such as Egypt or Babylon, but for him, there was only one God that mattered for him, one God that he worshipped. Just a footnote: about 500 years after Abraham, one of the pharaohs, Akhenaten, the father of the famous King Tut, outlawed polytheism and declared only Aten, the sun god, was to be worshipped. His son, King Tut, returned to the practice of polytheism.

This is a little story which I have told before. It gives something of a preview how Abraham would change the practice of many nations from polytheism to monotheism. This story is not in the Bible. It's found in

Jewish and Islamic literature. When Abraham was young he lived with his parents in Ur (an area in southern Iraq). Abraham's father made his living by making statues of the gods people worshipped in that area – and there were lots of gods (over 700 of them archeologists tell us) so he must have had a good business going. One day Abraham's father had to go on a business trip and he left Abraham in charge of the shop. Abraham felt disgusted with all those statues of gods and goddesses and broke them all – except for one he left standing in the corner of the shop. When his father came home and saw that all his statues were destroyed, he blamed Abraham and scolded him for it. Abraham denied doing it. He pointed to the god standing in the corner and said, "he did it."

In today's first reading, we hear Moses giving some last minute instructions to God's people before they enter the Promised Land. He tells them there is no other God than the Lord (Yahweh) and that only by being faithful to their God will they prosper. It's still good advice for today's world where polytheism and paganism have been replaced by atheism, hedonism and materialism.

HOMILY – I said in my introduction that Abraham and his descendants were an exception to the polytheism all around them. That's only partly true. Up until the Babylonian Exile, the Jews were often seduced into the worship of pagan gods while they continued to worship the God of Abraham. The first commandment "I am the Lord thy God, thou shalt not have strange gods before me" did not prevent the Jews giving in to the attractions of the gods of Canaan; for example, fertility gods who were honored by sacred prostitution and human sacrifice. It wasn't until the Babylonian Exile in 587 B.C. that the Jews finally began to get the message, that their God was the only God and there was no other. From that time the Jews remained loyal to the worship of their one God, in spite of a brief period in history when they were persecuted by the Greeks for refusing to worship Greek gods.

At the time of Jesus, the Jews were fiercely loyal to their own God. Jesus was a major challenge to what they believed. Jesus didn't show up saying I am God's Son so you must worship me too. The way he spoke and the things he did showed the power of God at work in him. He forgave sins. which was something only God could do; with authority he interpreted God's Law; he healed the sick and cast out demons; he could foretell the future; and he had power over nature – calming a storm, feeding a multitude, walking on water. He called God by the very intimate term, Abba, a term a son or daughter would use for father. He was ultimately put to death for the sin of blasphemy, claiming (or at least not denying) that he was the Christ (Messiah) the Son of the Blessed One. Then there was the ultimate miracle of his resurrection. Many wondered how he could be God's Son, which would make him divine, since there is only one God. For 300 years people tried to figure out Jesus, whether he is Son of God, whether he is some very unique person as the Arians claimed, whether he is a blasphemer. At the Council of Nicea (in modern day Turkey), after many heresies, war and much bloodshed, it was officially declared that Jesus is one in essence with God the Father, that Jesus is God but not the same person as the Father. Add to this Jesus' and Paul's teaching on the Holy Spirit and we have three divine persons, equal in power and majesty and yet united as one God. Thus we have the term Trinity, coined by Tertullian who lived around the year 200 and adopted by the council of Nicea in 325. We profess the Creed of

Nicea every Sunday. Because it was such a fiercely debated topic, the major portion of the Creed focuses on Jesus.

I have tried only to explain how the mystery came to be revealed, not how it can be. Yet we should not be surprised or dismayed that it is impossible for us to understand God. To fully understand God we would have to be as great as God, and we're not. We continue to discover mysteries about ourselves and nature all the time. There's still a lot we don't know. God gave us this knowledge because God wants us to know him, which is what lovers tend to do. So it's in love that God wants us to know him. Some day we will see for ourselves there is one God and that in God there are three persons, Father, Son and Holy Spirit. That is what faith is all about.

The Body and Blood of Christ
June 10, 2012

INTRODUCTION – (Exodus 24:3-8; Heb 9:11-15; Mark 14:12-16, 22-26) Our first reading is from the second book in the Bible, the Book of Exodus. The setting is in the desert of Sinai. God had just set his people free from their slavery in Egypt and Moses, as their leader, was bringing them to the Promised Land. Historically all this takes us back to the time of Ramses II, about 1250 to 1300 years before Christ. Today's first reading is one of the most important passages in the Old Testament. It tells us how God made a covenant with this rag-tag collection of ex-slaves, a solemn pact by which they would be his special people. In the covenant he promised them his special love and protection. We all know what promises the people made to God: we call them the Ten Commandments. Every facet of this reading is important, but as you will see from the other readings, today's liturgy focuses on the theme of blood. To make the covenant binding, Moses called for the sacrifice of young bulls. Half the blood from the sacrifice he sprinkled on the altar which represented God and the other half he sprinkled on the people. Blood was a symbol of life for the Jews. God and the people were thus bound together in a most solemn and serious bond. This covenant defined the Jews for centuries and much of the rest of the Bible pretty much describes the history of how God's people were either faithful or unfaithful to this covenant and the consequences that resulted from their fidelity or infidelity. Each day in prayer they recalled their special relationship with God and each year they solemnly celebrated this in the feast of Passover. Eventually the feast of Pentecost became a celebration of this covenant too.

The second reading from the Letter to the Hebrews assumes the recipients of this Letter knows all about the Jewish feast of Yom Kippur, the day of Atonement. After all, the letter is written to the Hebrews. Let me explain it for a few moments because you may not be very familiar with the Yom Kippur liturgy – which was very complex. I'm only going to explain the part of the liturgy that is relevant to today's second reading. Yom Kippur was the one day of the year that the High Priest was allowed to enter the Holy of Holies where the Arc of the Covenant was kept (until the Babylonians destroyed the Temple – then what happened to the Arc, no one knows). When the High Priest entered the Holy of Holies, he sprinkled the top of the Arc of the Covenant (called the mercy-seat), with the blood of animals that had been sacrificed. Here blood, which symbolized life, substituted for the sinful people who sought cleansing and reconciliation with God. It is as if the sinner laid down his or her life before God asking for his mercy through the blood of sacrificial animals. Assuming the reader knew all this, the Letter to the Hebrews tells us how Jesus entered into the eternal sanctuary, the highest heaven, the abode of God. Jesus entered with his own blood that he shed for us for the forgiveness of sins, an eternal and perfect sacrifice.

HOMILY – I said earlier the focus is on blood and how it was used by Moses to enact a covenant, binding the Jewish people to God and God to his people. That covenant was broken many times in the history of God's people, so much so that about 700 years later, God spoke through his prophet Jeremiah that he would make a new covenant with his people. "It will not be like the covenant I made with their fathers for they broke my covenant and I had to show myself their master this is the covenant which I will make says the Lord, I will place my law within them and write it upon their hearts; I will be their God and they shall be my people. All, from least to greatest, shall know me, says the Lord, for I will forgive their evildoing and remember their sin no more." (Jer. 31:31-34)

When he gave them the cup to drink from and told them: "this is my blood of the covenant," the Apostles would have been shocked. Jews could never, under any circumstances, drink blood or eat any meat with blood in it. Now Jesus tells them to drink it. The meaning would not have been lost on them: they were entering into a new covenant with Jesus and ultimately with God; they would be bound together in a relationship in which they would share in God's life – a relationship in which they would become a new creation and be purified of their sinfulness.

None of the gospel writers mention any of the special foods at the paschal meal they were celebrating. The focus is all on Jesus and the bread he gave, which he pronounced was his body, and the cup of wine, which he pronounced was his blood. After his death and resurrection, it gave them a way to remain united with him and he with them.

The Church teaches us that the bread and wine are truly changed and that we receive the whole Christ, the risen Christ, whether under the appearance of bread or wine. But we are reminded of the fuller meaning of our union with him and our covenant with him when we receive under both forms. We only advise people not to receive from the cup if they have a cold or sore throat.

Today is the feast of the Body and Blood of Christ. It is one of the biggest challenges Catholics have today because our culture seems not to believe something is real unless we see it for ourselves. However, with faith we can't use the motto: "seeing is believing." We have to reverse that motto to: "Believing is seeing," for if we take on faith what Jesus said, we will someday see it to be true. If you don't think Jesus made himself clear about the Eucharist, read the sixth chapter of John. We will read that chapter starting the last week of July and all through August. It's one of the most beautiful chapters in the gospels and it is something you don't want to miss.

11th Sunday in Ordinary Time
June 17, 2012

INTRODUCTION – (Ez 17:22-24; 2 Cor 5:6-10; Mark 4:26-34) Our first reading comes from the prophet Ezekiel. Ezekiel loved to use symbolism, either spoken or acted out, in order to get his message across. In today's reading he talks about trees. The first image is that God would take a cutting from a tree and plant it in Israel where it would grow into a majestic tree. This prophecy comes at the time of the Babylonian exile. Jerusalem's king and the leading citizens of Israel were captured by the Babylonians and taken off to Babylon. The king's sons were executed. It appeared to be the end of the Davidic monarchy. But God would raise up a future king from the house of David. This is the meaning of the topmost branch of the tree that God would take and replant in Israel. By this symbol, God was telling his people he was not giving up on them. Then other trees are mentioned. God brings low the high tree and lifts high the lowly tree. It is God who humbles the proud and mighty (Babylon and Egypt) and raises up the lowly. It is a message of hope to a people in despair and is meant to give God's people courage as they patiently wait for God to act on their behalf.

HOMILY – Today, I have a few one-liners in honor of our fathers. A mother brought her little four year-old son to the card store and told him to pick out a Fathers' Day card for his dad. He kept picking out cards and putting them back. She said, "can't you find one that you like." He said, "I'm looking for one with money in it." A little girl asked her dad, "why do you brag about wearing the pants in the family when it is mom who always tells you which pair to put on." One day a grandfather was visiting his family and his little grandchild asked him, "Can you croak like a frog?" Grandfather said, "I think I can do that. Why?" The little grandchild answered, "well dad said when you croak we're all going to Disneyland." A father was talking with his buddy about his kids. He said, "ever since my son was little I've been trying to teach him the value of a dollar. Now that he has begun to understand, he wants his allowance in gold." It's been just a little over 100 years since Father's day was first celebrated, but it took until 1972 for Congress to make it official. I am guessing it took so long because it was probably too difficult an item for Congress to handle. Some things just take time. It's what our gospel teaches us today.

Today we have two parables of Jesus from St. Mark. The first is about how seed grows and how the farmer has to patiently wait for it. This reminds us how, in our spiritual lives, we have to do some of the work. The farmer has to prepare the soil, plant the seed, keep the weeds down, maybe even fertilize it and water it, but we have to depend on God to do what we can't do. We have to be patient for God to do his part. St. Augustine said it so well: "we have to work as if everything depended on us and pray as if everything depended on God." We need God's help if we hope to be part of God's kingdom (which is what the parable is ultimately about). We remember Jesus told us, "without me you can do nothing."

The second parable about the mustard seed shows us that if we are patient and do depend on God, great things will take place. This parable connects with the first reading about the small branch of the cedar tree that grew into a majestic tree. Someone pointed out that if in 1965 you bought McDonald's stock for $22.50 and had purchased 100 shares, today it would be worth nearly 6 million dollars. Not bad. Consider the Church. Jesus began it with 12 men and a handful of faithful followers. Today it has grown to 1.2 billion members. That's pretty impressive too.

This past week I finished our next book for our book club entitled *Flunkin' Sainthood*. The author, Jana Riess, who will be with us at our next meeting, tells how she tried a variety of spiritual practices, devoting herself to each one for an entire month. For example, she fasted faithfully for a month, (she picked February for her time to fast because it is the shortest month), then she worked on contemplation, then being generous, being grateful, living the Sabbath like the Jews, praying the divine office, etc. She claims she failed each one – yet the overall effect of her efforts made a big difference in her attitude and in her life. By the end of the year, she had a greater peace and a new-found ability to forgive – especially her father who abandoned her family when she was young. Comparing her experience to today's gospel, she planted a few seeds herself. She felt many did not take root, but the ones that did brought her abundant blessings. Besides being quite humorous, her book was a good illustration of today's gospel. Briefly, Jesus tells us don't try to be holy without his help, have a lot of patience with yourself and with God's working, and expect great blessings if you do what you can do to get closer to God. Amen.

12th Sunday in Ordinary Time
June 25, 2006

HOMILY – (Job 38:1, 8-11; 2 Cor. 5:14-17; Mark 4:35-41) Four hunters were out tramping through the woods looking for deer. Suddenly a large buck jumped out of the bushes and they all fired at once. The deer fell down dead, but when they examined it it was only hit by one bullet. They couldn't' figure out whose bullet had killed the deer and while they were arguing over it a game warden came by. They asked him to help them figure out who brought down the deer. After examining it he asked whether there was a preacher in the group. One of the men said he was and the game warden said the deer was his. They were amazed at his answer and asked how he had figured that out. The game warden said, well the deer was killed with only one bullet and it went in one ear and out the other.

God did not reveal the concept of reward and punishment, heaven and hell, in the next life until about a century or two before the time of Christ. Prior to that time they thought that when a person died, the soul went to a place somewhere down below the surface of the earth called Sheol. Sheol was a place where nothing much ever happened. The spirit of a person experienced neither happiness nor unhappiness there. At the same time, God's people firmly believed that God was just and fair, that God rewarded good people and punished bad people. Because they had no clue that reward or punishment could occur after this life, they logically concluded that, since God is fair, God rewards us in this life if we're good or punishes us in this life if we're bad. The logical conclusion to that kind of theology is that if we look at a person and see they are prosperous, healthy, happy, and blessed in numerous ways, that is a sign they are a really virtuous and holy person. Conversely, if a person is having problems, if they are poor, or suffer from physical sickness, or suffer in some other way, they must be being punished for some evil in their life, even if they themselves are unaware of anything evil they might have done. But they were smart enough to know things didn't always work that way. Sometimes bad things happened to good people while other people got away with murder. These everyday realities must have caused a real crisis of faith for many good people at that time.

The book of Job tries to explore this dilemma. Job is a very holy and good man. Even God admits it at the beginning of the book. He is blessed in every way. But by a few sudden tragedies he loses his crops, his livestock, his lands, the respect of his peers, and all of his sons and daughters. His wife and a few faithful friends kept telling him he must deserve all this for something he did. Most of us are familiar with his initial view of what was happening to him when he declared: "the Lord gives and the Lord takes away." People often speak of the "patience of Job," but even his patience wore thin and he started asking for answers, or rather I should say he started demanding answers as to why he was suffering all these things.

God's response to his demands came in the form of questions, questions mostly about the mysteries of nature, questions like we hear in today's first reading such as "who has power over the sea and the waves." These questions go on for four chapters as God asks Job how the stars were put in place, how the clouds are formed, what causes the wind to blow, who feeds the fish in the depths of the sea, or how do the animals in the wild live. These questions were meant to lead the readers of the book of Job to a sense of trust that God is in control of all things. Even if we don't understand or know what he's doing, he knows, and we just have to trust him.

Through the life, death and resurrection of Jesus we have been given more insights, more answers, more help to our faith and to the mystery of suffering than Job was able to come up with. And yet, many of us still tend to think about life the way that people long before Jesus did. At least subconsciously we think if we are good, God should make life pleasant for us and if other people are bad (not us of course!) God should not let them get by with it. Sometimes that's the way things happen. A good life does have many rewards and an evil life usually catches up with a person, but it doesn't always happen right away. And when life doesn't go the way we think it should, our faith is shaken. We don't understand how God works. We are somewhat like the apostles in today's gospel, when storms come up we cry out, "Lord, don't you care that we are going to drown?"

In each Sunday's liturgy, in Communion, in our prayers, God gives us as many answers as he thinks we can understand right now. We have the good news that God loves us so much that he sent his only Son to teach us, to heal us and to suffer and die for us. We have the resurrection which gives us hope that sin and evil and suffering will not have the last word. We have the Eucharist which tells us that in our journey through life God will not abandon us, but will always be with us to strengthen us and unite us closely with himself. The answers we get, like the answers Job got, continue to require us to have faith. Jesus asked the apostles in today's gospel, "Why are you so terrified? Why are you so lacking in faith?" Jesus asks us those same questions today. As I meditated on this gospel, I wondered how the apostles might have responded if Jesus had asked those questions before he calmed the storm. Think about that for a moment. If he did, do you think they would have heard him? It probably would have gone in one ear and out the other as they would have been too worried about the storm. It's easy for anyone to see we should have trusted more after danger has past, but our Lord wants us to hear this question also when the storm is raging and the waves are high. God wants us to know he is still in control, even though we may wonder, "how can he be?"

Birth of John the Baptist
June 24, 2012

INTRODUCTION – (Is 49:1-6; Acts 13:22-26; Lk 1:57-66, 80) We are familiar with John the Baptist from the readings during Advent. John was the prophet who immediately preceded Jesus and foretold his coming. John's birthday usually falls on a weekday, but it is considered such an important feast that when it falls on Sunday, it takes precedence over the Sunday readings. If you are curious why the feast of his birth is today, consider this. The feast of the Annunciation is celebrated on March 25. When the archangel Gabriel appeared to Mary, the archangel told her that her cousin Elizabeth was already in her sixth month. So add three months to March 25 and we are at June 25. (Since John's birthday is the 24th – he must have come a day early).

The liturgy usually puts the feast day of saints on the day they died and entered into eternal life. But there are only three birthdays. This is because their birth is considered especially holy since they were born free from any sin.

[eve] – Our first reading is from Jeremiah, a prophet who lived 600 years before Christ. As God was telling Jeremiah he was to be a prophet, the reading describes that role. This description of a prophet fits John the Baptist as well.

The gospel is the annunciation to John's father, the old priest Zechariah, that he and his elderly wife would have a child, a special child who would prepare God's people for the coming of the Messiah.

[morning] – In today's first reading, the prophet Second Isaiah, who lived about 500 years before Christ, speaks of some mysterious person who was identified simply as God's servant. This poem and three others in Isaiah's writings are known as Servant Songs. The early Church found these songs described Jesus in a most uncanny way. They are usually read during Holy Week. Today, however, the liturgy applies this second of the Servant Songs to John the Baptist because it states: "the Lord called me from birth, from my mother's womb he gave me my name."

When the archangel Gabriel had appeared to John's father Zachariah nine months earlier, he told him his wife Elizabeth would have a son and he was to be named John. Zachariah and Elizabeth were a very old couple and Zachariah didn't believe the angel. Not smart! He lost the ability to speak because of his lack of faith. (It's like the angel was telling him, "keep your mouth shut and your lack of faith to yourself.") Once Zachariah gave his child the name he had been told to name him, he showed he fully accepted all that the angel told him and his ability to speak returned.

HOMILY – Since I gave a long introduction, I do not have a very long sermon. One of Aesop's most famous fables is the story of the ant and the grasshopper.

The story goes like this: In a field one summer's day, a Grasshopper was hopping about, chirping and singing to its heart's content. An Ant passed by, bearing along with great toil a kernel of corn he was taking to the nest. "Why not come and chat with me," said the Grasshopper, "instead of toiling and moiling in that way?" "I am helping to lay up food for the winter," said the Ant, "and recommend you to do the same." "Why bother about winter?" said the Grasshopper; we have got plenty of food at present." The Ant went on its way and continued its toil. When the winter came, the Grasshopper had no food and found itself dying of hunger, while it saw the ants distributing corn and grain from the stores they had collected in the summer. Then the Grasshopper knew: "It is best to prepare for the days of necessity."

Even 2500 years ago, people knew the importance of preparing for the future. It's still just as true today. If we do not learn this lesson when life is good, we'll learn the hard way when it's too late. This goes for education, investing, health and all kinds of important areas of life.

John the Baptist's role in life was to insist on the need to prepare. He called people to repent and prepare for the coming of God's kingdom. His message is as important today as it ever was. There is a kind of new age theology that follows the attitude of the Grasshopper. It says don't worry. Everybody is going to be in heaven in the end (except for someone like Hitler). Although God wants all people to be saved, there are abundant passages in the Scriptures that warn us that we cannot take salvation for granted. Jesus, who came to save us and who revealed to us so clearly the love of God, warned us: "The door to heaven is narrow. Work hard to get in, because many will try to enter and will not be able." (Luke 13:23) Jesus' message at the beginning of his ministry was the same message as John the Baptist: "repent and believe in the gospel." The word "believe" means more than saying, "I believe." It means putting our belief into action. Statistics keep coming out that fewer and fewer people are coming to Church, which is an indication that more and more people believe that worship of God is not all that important. I think it's the entitlement mentality. We feel entitled to be happy (even eternally), no matter what we do or how we live. That's not what the Scriptures tell us. I think the most important lesson we can learn from this feast of John the Baptist is to prepare. The fact you are here today is one good sign that you understand we need to prepare to meet our God. Amen.

13th Sunday in Ordinary Time
July 1, 2012

INTRODUCTION – The first reading (Wisdom 1:13-15, 2:23-24; 2 Cor. 8:7, 9, 13-15; Mark 5:21-43) tells us God did not make death. Rather, it came about through the envy of the devil. This is obviously a commentary on the story of Adam and Eve in the garden – how they tried to find their happiness and fulfillment by making their own rules rather than doing what God told them to do or not do. They thought God wanted to prevent them from being happy instead of trusting that God had their best interests at heart. When the devil convinces us we need to do things our way and not God's way in order to find happiness, we find death instead. The two miracles in today's gospel (Mark 5:21-43) show us what can happen when people really put their trust in Jesus. The second reading is an appeal to the Corinthians (2 Cor. 8:7, 9, 13-15) for financial help for the poor in Jerusalem.

HOMILY – While our government will now be providing health care for many more people, our gospel today tells us not to forget that God too is interested in our well-being. Today in the gospel he shows us the blessings that come to those who have faith in him.

Today, and the next couple of weeks, we will hear more about Jesus' healings. Today's gospel is one of the most detailed descriptions we find in the gospels of Jesus' healing work. Next week we hear something very surprising about Jesus when he goes to his hometown of Nazareth. Mark tells us because of their lack of faith there, Jesus "was not able to perform any mighty deeds there – apart from curing a few sick people." The following week we heard about Jesus sending his Apostles to the nearby villages to drive out demons and to heal the sick. They anointed the sick with oil and cured them. The oil is a detail only Mark tells us about. The use of oil to heal the sick is also mentioned in the Letter of James. James says, "is anyone sick among you, he should call for the priests of the Church and let the priests pray over them anointing them with oil in the name of the Lord. The prayer of faith will save the sick persons, and the Lord will raise them up. If they have committed any sins, their sins will be forgiven them." (James 5:14-15) So, for three weeks we are going to hear about Jesus' healing ministry. There is an insert in the bulletin that says more about healing and because our gospels focus on it, I intend to have the anointing of the sick next Sunday after all the Masses.

There are two details in today's gospel I've never noticed before, and I want to point them out to you. Notice Jesus does not pray over people when he heals them. Usually he touches them or just speaks a word to them and they are healed. In the Acts of the Apostles, we read when the Apostles healed anyone they did it in the name of Jesus or in the name of the Lord. The Letter of James tells people if they are sick to call for the priests of the Church and the priests will pray over them anointing them in the name of the Lord. Jesus certainly prayed a lot – but he didn't pray over people when he wanted to heal them. He didn't need to invoke anyone's name or ask anyone's intercession for he did it by his own authority and power.

The second detail I want to point out is this: The woman with the constant flow of blood was considered unclean by Jewish law. That doesn't mean she was sinful, although the ordinary person at that time would probably have thought that God was punishing her for something evil she had done. That was their thinking. The condition of being unclean simply meant a person was not allowed to participate in public religious activities such as going to the Temple. If anyone touched a person who was unclean, such as a leper or a dead person, then they became unclean. They were unclean until they were purified – usually by a ceremonial bath. The woman with the flow of blood would have been considered unclean, just as if she had leprosy, and anyone who had contact with her, even if by accident, would become unclean. There was a superstitious belief at the time that if a person with healing powers touched or was touched by a person who was unclean, the person with spiritual powers would lose their power. Thus the woman in the gospel had this dilemma, she thought contact with Jesus the healer would heal her, but her contact with him might destroy his power to heal. If she asked him to touch her, he might refuse. So, as we are told, she secretly touched his garment. "Instead of uncleanness passing from the woman to Jesus, healing power flows from Jesus to the woman." (Joel Marcus, Mark 1-8, pg 367) This same flow of healing power brought Jairus' daughter back to life.

The word "save" is a very important concept here. It has a surface meaning and a deeper meaning. The root meaning is "to rescue from danger." On the surface, it means a release from chronic or life-threatening illness. On a deeper level, it means God rescuing a person from the realm of the dead or from the sufferings that will come at the end of time. One cannot read this story about Jesus raising Jairus' daughter back to life without being reminded of Jesus own resurrection. Especially is this true if you were reading the gospel in the original Greek for the same words are used; Jesus tells the girl to rise, just as he will be raised and she arises just as he will arise from death after three days. We are, in our modern day world, blessed with wonderful health care workers. But we can't think we can get along without Jesus. There are limits to what doctors and nurses can do. We are not going to live in this world forever. God made us for better things. Jesus can help us with our everyday problems if we come to him and have faith in him, but only Jesus can help us in the most profound sense of the word "save." Jesus' death and resurrection is a definitive triumph over death and evil and it is our way to salvation and eternal peace. Amen.

Fourteenth Sunday of Ordinary Time
July 8, 2012

INTRODUCTION – (Ezekiel 2:2-5; 2 Cor. 12:7-10; Mark 6:1-6) Sometimes prophets predicted the future, but most of the time their task was to remind God's people of how God wanted them to live. Their efforts were not always appreciated by the people who heard the message. The prophet Ezekiel lived about 600 years before Christ. He had to warn the people of the national disaster that was headed their way if they did not change their ways. In the beginning of his book he describes, as much as it is possible, a vision of God in heaven. He was so overwhelmed he fell flat onto the ground. This is where our first reading comes in. God got him back on his feet and commissioned him to be a prophet. God cautions Ezekiel that as a prophet he would not have an easy job of it. The passage prepares us for the gospel that tells of Jesus, the greatest prophet of all, who was rejected by his own people when he came to preach in his hometown of Nazareth.

HOMILY – Sullivan went to his favorite race track and after a couple of races, he noticed on that particular day a priest was there who always went to one of the horses that would be running in the next race and gave that horse a blessing. Sullivan noticed too that the horse that had been blessed always won. For several races he watched this with great interest. It happened every time. Finally, for the last race, Sullivan decided to bet everything he had on the particular horse he saw the priest had blessed. As the horses were racing around the track, the horse Sullivan bet on dropped dead. Sullivan couldn't believe his bad luck and went up to the priest. He told the priest, "I watched you bless every one of the winning horses, so I bet everything I had on this last race, and that horse dropped dead. What happened? The priest looked at him, shook his head and said: "you must not be Catholic because you don't know the difference between a blessing and the Last Rites."

The sacrament of the sick we are offering today used to be called the "Last Rites," or "Extreme Unction." That's because people forgot the primary purpose of that sacrament is originally and principally a blessing for a sick person. During the Middle Ages, theologians began stressing the spiritual effects of this sacrament as a preparation for a person to meet our Lord in death, and its main purpose (for the healing of the sick) was relegated to a secondary position. I remember times how embarrassed I would be to stand at the death bed of a 96 year old man or woman who definitely was dying and who was looking forward to being free of his or her suffering and in administrating this sacrament of the anointing I would have to be saying prayers that that person would soon be up and about, ready to resume their former duties. In other words, the prayers that were part of this sacrament were always prayers for healing, but the current theology at the time was to wait until a person was very near death before they received the sacrament. Sometimes the priest wasn't called until it was too late. This was one of the things the Vatican Council did – to re-emphasize the primary purpose of this sacrament and started calling it by its real name: The Sacrament of the Anointing of the Sick. I have a great deal of faith in the power of this sacrament. It is my custom whenever I visit someone who is sick, whether in the hospital or a nursing home or at home, I usually give them the Anointing of the Sick. It is still administered to those who are dying, but there are special prayers for a dying person and I no longer have to pray that a 96-year old grannie is soon able to resume her former duties.

Faith is important as we receive it, faith that in this sacrament Jesus is touching us, that's all the faith we need. This does not necessarily mean we have to have faith that he will cure us, and that if we're not cured then it's our fault because we didn't have enough faith. Some of the faith healers on TV give that impression. You might even get that impression from St. Mark's gospel today. He tells us Jesus was unable to perform any mighty deeds in his hometown apart from curing a few sick people because of their lack of faith. (That is, they didn't have faith in him as God's prophet!) I'm sure there aren't many people who have more faith than St. Paul had. Yet look at today's second reading. St. Paul suffered some "thorn in the flesh." In the next sentence, Paul talks about weakness. You might think it was some kind of physical ailment, but we don't know for sure. Some scholars believe it is the daily worry and care of the Churches he founded that he is referring to. Whoever can say what it was for sure has the answer to the proverbial $64,000 question. The important lesson to learn from this reading is that in spite of Paul's prayers to God that God relieve him of it, God did not. God simply said, "My grace is sufficient for you, for power is made perfect in weakness." I believe what this means is that sometimes our sufferings can be a blessing to us, although it may not seem that way at the time. I know when I was a child I suffered asthma for many years, and as I see it now, I know that suffering brought me closer to God. We need to have faith with any sacrament, faith that Jesus loves us, faith that he hears us, faith that in some way that sacrament will bring God's blessing and grace to us. It may not be the exact blessing we think we want; it may be a blessing God thinks we need.

Actually, sometimes Jesus healed people who had no faith at all. For example, when he raised the son of a widow back to life. It happened simply as he was walking toward the town of Naim. He encountered a funeral procession coming in the opposite direction. He stopped the procession and raised the dead person, the son of a widowed mother. Or in John's gospel, Jesus came up to a man who had been crippled for 38 years and just told him to get up and walk. Jesus was immediately lost in the crowd before the man even got to know who it was who cured him. But usually Jesus says, "your faith has saved you" after he heals someone. I think in the final analysis, faith is putting into God's hands what we can't control and believing always that he's with us, that he's interested in our welfare and that he loves us. Amen.

Fifteenth Sunday of Ordinary Time
July 15, 2012

INTRODUCTION – (Amos 7:12-15; Ephesians 1:3-10; Mark 6:7-13) Sometimes prophets predicted the future but most of the time they tried to direct God's people to live by God's laws. Consequently, those who were not living according to God's laws usually did not appreciate the prophet's reproach. Our first reading today is taken from the Book of the Prophet Amos. Amos lived over 700 years before Christ. At that time and in that culture there were professional prophets who made their living by telling people how to solve their problems, giving them advice, predicting the future, etc. These professionals were often servants of pagan gods and they did not speak for the God of Abraham. They usually spoke the kinds of things their clients would be pleased to hear because if they offended their client they would not have been paid their fee. When Amos went to Bethel, where there was a temple in competition with the true Temple in Jerusalem, Amos did not have comforting things to say to the people about the way they were living. He warned them of great disaster they would suffer if they didn't change their ways. The high priest of the Bethel sanctuary, Amaziah, mistook him for one of the professional prophets and told him to get out of town. Amos protested that he was not a career prophet, rather he was living a nice peaceful life as a farmer and God called him to go to Bethel and warn the people that their sinful lives would lead to destruction. Today's passage prepares us for the gospel where Jesus sends his apostles out to preach and warns them that their message may not always be well received.

HOMILY – Last week's gospel told us of Jesus' rejection by his relatives, friends and neighbors in his hometown of Nazareth. Today, Jesus is preparing his apostles to go out for the first time to announce God's kingdom by healing and casting out demons. It could be a difficult assignment. The job of telling people they need to repent and change their ways is not always popular. John the Baptist had some success in preaching repentance, but most of us know what happened to him. Jesus and his apostles would also have known what happened to the Baptist. So he warns his apostles to move on if they are not accepted. They should even shake the dust of the town from their sandals.

A number of themes suggest themselves in today's gospel; for example, the theme of the rejection of the true prophet of God such as happened to Amos and John the Baptist and Jesus, the greatest of all prophets who came to teach us God's ways. There are many other topics that would be worth dwelling on, but let me get to the one that occupied my reflections on the gospel this week – the theme of simplicity. In today's gospel, we have no details as to where the apostles were to go, how long they would be gone, or what Jesus was going to do in the meantime. We are given a lot of detail about what they were allowed to take with them – one tunic, sandals and a walking staff. (Luke does not even allow a walking staff and Matthew does not allow either the staff or the sandals). Jesus wanted them to learn to trust God to care for their needs. In the light of this austerity, I examined myself – as I believe St. Mark wants his hearers to do. I trust in God, but I reflect on all the stuff I take with me when I just take a day off, not to mention all the other stuff I surround myself with, especially books and closets full of stuff. We are a society with lots of stuff. There is an insert in today's bulletin on living simply. One of the things we see in many people who want to live a life centered on God, such as hermits and monks and people like St. Benedict and St. Francis and St. Dominic, is that they try to live very simple lives. So many things can get in the way of our spiritual growth, especially the TV. I seldom have mine on, and I seldom miss it, unless when I want to see the news. I do admit, however, of having lots of clutter and I've read a couple of books on how to reduce clutter, but I don't have time to do it. That's another area where we all have a lot of clutter: our busy schedules. It's important that we don't keep ourselves so busy that we don't have time to pray. In our busy-ness we have to keep in mind what our priorities are or we will find ourselves going around in circles. God should be our highest priority.

Maybe St. Francis could follow the gospel literally, but in our society people will probably keep wearing shoes and changing their clothes occasionally. In order to get to church, most everyone here needs a car (and it's nice if you have a check book too). Few of us have neighbors who will invite us to dinner every night, so we need food and a roof over our heads (especially in the winter). It doesn't get so cold in the Middle East and the apostles lived in a culture where hospitality was automatically offered, so they could survive on less.

However, I do want to mention four things we can especially do without as we make this journey through life: ONE is guilt. Guilt can be healthy or unhealthy. Healthy guilt is something we feel when we have failed to live up to our ideals and our values. When we fail, there is a way of taking care of that. We ask forgiveness. If we have offended against our spiritual ideals, we ask forgiveness of God and start over. Sometimes we don't forgive ourselves and thus we keep our traveling bag always full of guilt. When God forgives us, we have to forgive ourselves. The SECOND thing we need to get rid of is unforgiveness of others. Some people just hold on to grudges forever. The grudges we hold on to usually hurt us more than the people we are angry with. Remember when we pray, we pray that God forgives us as we forgive others. A THIRD thing is fear and worry. Fear helps us prepare for problems and prepare ourselves how to deal with them and in that it is healthy. But some people worry about everything - most of which they can't do anything about. Jesus asks us to have more trust in God as we travel this road of life. LAST but not least, get rid of ingratitude, especially toward God. We need to thank God daily for his blessings, and that's what brings us here today – to say Thanks. Amen.

Sixteenth Sunday of Ordinary Time
July 22, 2012

INTRODUCTION – (Jeremiah 23:1-6; Ephesians, 2:13-18; Mk. 6:30-34) Our first reading is from Jeremiah the prophet who lived about 600 years before Christ. As I explain the reading, I'll begin by explaining the second half. Jeremiah pronounces a solemn promise from God that begins with the words: "The days are coming says the Lord" The promise that follows these words is a promise meant to give hope to God's people who had been scattered by the Babylonian invasion. It would be many days before God's promise would be fulfilled – 50 years before the people could return to their homeland from Babylon and almost 600 years before the king whom God promises would arrive. We know the promised king was Jesus the Christ, an offspring of David who ruled God's people with wisdom, establishing justice and security in the land. We still wait and pray for the promise of justice and security to be fulfilled. The first part of our reading uses an image that goes back almost 4000 years where the king was referred to as shepherd of his people. In the kingdoms of Israel and Judah, the king was considered to be the shepherd of God's people. Most of the time the kings of Israel and Judah did not rule according to God's laws. The gospel applies the same image of shepherd to Jesus who will faithfully lead God's people as God desires.

HOMILY – Last week's gospel ended with Jesus sending his apostles out to preach repentance, drive out demons and heal the sick. In today's gospel, they return to Jesus to report how their mission went. Jesus recognized they all had a need for some rest and some quiet time. They were no doubt looking forward to just having him to themselves for a little while, but that did not happen. Jesus and his apostles had stirred up a great spiritual hunger and hope in many people and they came looking for their hunger to be satisfied. We notice that when the people found Jesus, he was not annoyed or too busy to for them. He was moved with compassion for they were like sheep without a shepherd. Jesus, first of all, satisfies their spiritual hunger by teaching them, giving them directions on how to live, how to love God and one another, encouraging them, perhaps helping them to understand the meaning of their lives. Today's gospel is also preparing us for what is to follow, where we will hear in the next few weeks how Jesus satisfied their physical hunger in the multiplication of the loaves and fishes.

Two ideas struck me as worthy of our reflection. Think how privileged the apostles were to have Jesus with them all the time. We have Jesus with us all the time too. But as St. Augustine famously said in his book, the Confessions, when he came to know Jesus: "You were with me, but I was not with you." Like the apostles, we need to take time off just to be alone with him. We are doing that right now but going to Mass on the weekend is a minimum. I believe we also need to take time during the week. Without spending some quality time with Jesus during the week, the weekend Mass may not be so meaningful for us. Besides my daily Mass and the saying of the Divine Office, I usually try to spend an hour a day in some form of quiet prayer such as the rosary, or studying the Scriptures or just sitting quietly in Church. This is a great privilege for me and having this opportunity has been a great blessing for me.

The second idea worthy of our reflection is expressed in the last words of today's gospel: the people were like sheep without a shepherd and he began to teach them. Seeing Jesus as the good shepherd is one of the most popular ways to imagine him and one of the earliest ways Jesus was portrayed in Christian art. Psalm 23, "the Lord is my Shepherd," is the best known and best loved of all the 150 psalms. Having Jesus as our shepherd presupposes we allow him to lead us; in other words, we allow him to teach us and continue to teach us. We are never finished learning from him. Many, many people in our culture went to Catholic schools. Some continue to stay active in their faith and others have put it in a drawer with their diploma and forgotten about it. This group feels as if they know all they need to know about religion. They are like some of the students I taught when I taught high school religion. Often students would complain, "why are we studying this stuff, we learned this in grade school." It's as if you can come to know all you need to know about Jesus with a few little lessons. We're never finished learning. I love this quote from St. John of the Cross: "We must dig deeply in Christ. He is like a rich mine with many pockets containing treasures: however deep we dig we will never find their end or their limit. Indeed, in every pocket new seams of fresh riches are discovered on all sides."

For myself, I continue to be fascinated with the scriptures and continue to learn from them, even after studying them for over 50 years. You could say that I'm just a slow learner – and that may be true – but it's also true that we can never exhaust the riches we can discover as we come to know our Lord more and more deeply.

Jesus teaches us in many different ways, not just through the Scriptures. He teaches us in our daily prayers and meditation, in the Mass, in our interaction with others, in the saints, through the teachings of the Church, through spiritual books, even through the difficult challenges that life brings us. We call ourselves disciples. The word disciple means learner. When we've quit learning, we've quit being a disciple. The last line in today's gospel tells me: if we want to have Jesus as our shepherd, then we must allow him to be our teacher. Jesus saw the people like sheep without a shepherd – so how did he shepherd them – "he began to teach them many things."

Seventeenth Sunday of Ordinary Time
July 29, 2012

HOMILY – (2 Kings 4:42-44; Eph 4:1-6; John 6:1-15) Last week's gospel told us Jesus and his disciples tried to get away for a little while from their ministry of teaching and healing so they could get some rest. But somehow the crowd found him. He was not annoyed or angry that he and his disciples were going to miss out on this well-needed time to rest. Rather, he saw the crowd as sheep without a shepherd and he began to teach them many things. After meeting their spiritual needs, Jesus knew they had gone a long time without eating. So Jesus provides what the people needed for their empty stomachs.

Many people have asked, "did this really happen?" Because we have no details how it happened, many have tried to deny there was anything miraculous about what Jesus did and they invent some natural explanation of what took place. The story is presented to us as something awesome and marvelous. We just have to take it on faith. It is clear from all that we know that if something memorable and miraculous did not occur when Jesus fed 5000 people with five barley loaves and two fish, then we might as well deny all the other miracles in the gospels too. I say this because there is no other miracle in the gospels (except for the resurrection of Jesus himself) that is so well attested to and confirmed as genuine. It is the only miracle (again except for Jesus' resurrection) that is found in all four gospels. You might notice that John's gospel does not use the word "miracle." He calls it a sign as we heard today: "when the people saw the sign he had done." A sign is something that seeks to communicate some deeper reality to us. John is very explicit and expansive about what the multiplication of the loaves and fishes is trying to tell us. During this year (liturgically called "year B") most of our gospels are taken from St. Mark. At this point, however, we leave St. Mark and for five weeks, counting this week, we will reflect on St. John's much longer version of the multiplication of the loaves and fishes and what it all means. This is one of the most beautiful chapters in the gospel as far as I am concerned.

I do have some other items I want to talk about today. Starting with a personal item, I have acquired an additional responsibility. I have been appointed as Parochial Administrator of St. Leo for three months. I have been assured it will not involve much additional work. The pastor, Fr. Jim Schutte, is going away for three months to study. There is a priest who will say Mass there during that time. I tell you this so you don't have to hear about it by way of rumor.

Another item concerns our regular finances. Since our increased offertory support program a year ago, we have been doing well. I just want to offer everyone a great big thank you. We have a finance statement for the past fiscal year in today's bulletin. The extra money that put us ahead this year will help with our painting the church and with making up for the losses we suffered in the past three years. I am immensely grateful for your generosity.

Finally, I want to say something about the painting. The painters were hoping to start with the choir loft and move forward, but scheduling with the scaffolding company has run into a few snags, so until we get more scaffolding up the painters have been working on some of the lower walls. You can see some difference in the two transepts. All of the pews that have to be taken up to make room for scaffolding will be returned, except for the six that have been permanently removed to provide a gathering space in the back of church. It has become more popular to have funeral visitations in church before the funeral and we do not have enough room to accommodate many people with our small vestibule. Also, in bad weather, sometimes after a Mass or a wedding people may want to stay and visit for several minutes. When I came to St. Boniface 20 years ago, I asked people to remain silent before Mass for those who want to pray and to feel free to visit if they wanted to stay afterwards. People have been very considerate about keeping that practice and I am grateful.

I discovered a week ago that the church is actually far dirtier than I was aware. I guess I shouldn't be surprised after 50 years with candles constantly burning and sending their carbon up into the air. One of the workers recently took a ladder up to the gold leaf dome, just to check it out. It is gold leaf. He took a dozen or so dry cotton balls and just rubbed it over the gold. This is what he got. (show very blackened cotton balls) Then he went over the spot with a dry cleaning sponge and got more dirt. It's an expensive project but our church is a sacred place to be honored and respected and it is our place to pray each day the greatest prayer we have.

There is one other thing. A few weeks ago a very generous parishioner called to make an offer. This parishioner said if we had a capital campaign for the church painting, that person would match every dollar that was donated up to $50,000 dollars. You will receive a letter about this matching gift this week. I could not let this opportunity slip by. I hope our parishioners can come up with $50,000 (or more), then (somewhat like the loaves and fishes on a smaller scale), it will be multiplied and we will receive an additional $50,000 to help us out. When I first heard about this offer, I told a friend of mine and within a day he gave me a check for $5000. So, I just need nine more people like that. Please, I ask you if you would read carefully the letter I am sending and consider helping us this way.

Eighteenth Sunday of Ordinary Time
August 5, 2012

INTRODUCTION – (Ex 16:2-4, 12-15; Eph 4:17, 20-24; John 6:24-35) Last Sunday's gospel was about Jesus feeding a great multitude of over 5000 people with five loaves of bread and two fish. The people were so impressed by this miracle that they wanted to make him their king. The idea may have been tempting to Jesus, perhaps thinking that as king he may have greater influence on a greater number of people, thus facilitating the coming of God's kingdom. Yet, he knew his Father had a different plan, one that went beyond giving people free food. His mission was to change hearts, a mission that would cause the political and religious leaders of his day to feel as if he was threatening their power and position. The disciples, of course, would have been excited about Jesus being king (it would enhance their social status), so he sent them off in their boat, away from the enthusiastic crowd. He slipped away from everyone and went to a mountain alone to pray. Jesus rejoined his apostles as they were traveling across the sea to Capernaum. He came to them walking on the water. Today's gospel continues with the people catching up with Jesus at Capernaum.

Since the gospel recalls how God fed his people with Manna 1300 years earlier, as they were leaving Egypt and were traveling through the desert to get to the promised land our first reading is from Exodus where that event is described.

HOMILY – We could analyze today's gospel verse by verse and it would have so much to say to us. However, to make it simple, I want to focus on just two verses.

The first verse is Jesus' words: "Amen, amen I say to you, you are looking for me not because you saw signs but because you ate the loaves and were filled." The key word here is "signs." In last weeks' gospel, St. John tells us a large crowd was following Jesus because they saw the signs he was performing in healing the sick. John also tells us after the people saw the sign he had done in feeding the multitude, they wanted to make him a king. Here Jesus says the people were looking for him not because they saw signs but because they got a free meal. Signs, however, are not always crystal clear. Of course, we know what a "stop" sign is telling us. But if you are driving in London during rush hour, as I did once, I found the signs were more confusing than helpful. When we look at the clouds, for example, we might not be sure what they are telling us; will there be some rain, a lot of rain, a serious storm or will the clouds just pass over and the sun will shine? What does the mysterious smile of the Mona Lisa say to us? Words are signs, but if they were always clear, there would never be any miscommunication. Jesus worked a sign, but the people grasped it only on one level, the material level. They saw an easy future for themselves, they would be provided for, free food for the rest of their lives, perhaps also thrown in for good measure, they would have a leader that would liberate them from their hated Roman rulers. That's not what Jesus' sign meant. Jesus wanted to feed and nourish them – not, however, on a material level. He would feed their minds, their hearts, their spirits for all eternity. As he says later in John's gospel: "I came that they may have life and may have it to the full." (Jn. 10:10) A lifetime supply of fish sandwiches may satisfy our physical need, but we have deeper needs than that. The crowd wasn't thinking about those deeper needs, and that's what Jesus needed to explain to them. How many people in today's world do not think about their deep spiritual needs either and all they think of are their material needs? Our spiritual needs are just as practical as our physical needs. Remember, our Lord tells us: "One does not live by bread alone, but by every word that comes forth from the mouth of God." (Mt. 4:4) Jesus is being totally practical. Nothing is more practical than finding God it changes our whole life.

The second verse I propose we reflect on: "This is the work of God, that you believe in the one he sent." Here the key word is "work." Faith is work. So many people expect faith to be easy – just say I believe. They expect once they say: "I believe," peace, love and joy will come flowing into their hearts. It works that way, sometimes. Other times following Christ means carrying a cross. "Whoever wishes to come after me must deny himself, take up his cross, and follow me." (Mt. 16:24) The hard work comes when we accept him on his terms. Too often we try to follow him on our terms. Like the people who got the free meal, we are willing to recognize him as our Lord and king when he does what we want. It's work, however, to get up on Sunday morning when we would rather stay in bed; it's work to resist temptation; it's work to forgive people who have hurt us; it's work accepting some of the crosses that come our way. Although we might say that believing in Jesus and following him is work, when we do give our lives over to him completely, believing in him and following him comes easier, for we will not be left to carry our cross alone. He will be with us always. Only he can fulfill our deepest hunger. Amen.

Nineteenth Sunday of Ordinary Time
August 12, 2012

INTRODUCTION – (1 Kings 19:4-8; Eph. 4:30-5:2; John 6:41-51) Jezebel was an evil queen who reigned in Israel eight hundred fifty years before Christ. One of her many goals in life was to eliminate faith and worship of Yahweh, the God of Israel. At the same time, there also lived in Israel the prophet Elijah who was dedicated to serving Yahweh. Naturally, these two would collide. Elijah had just finished working a powerful miracle on Mt. Carmel, a place now known as Haifa, which dramatically demonstrated that Yahweh was truly God, and that the gods Jezebel promoted were non-existent. Jezebel, instead of being converted, became a sore loser. She sent her army after Elijah to kill him. Elijah quickly left the place. He ran to the desert in southern Judea and this is where we meet him in today's first reading. He is hungry, tired and deeply depressed. You will hear in today's reading that God did not desert his faithful prophet. The mountain of God, Horeb, which we will hear mentioned is also Mt. Sinai, the mountain where God gave Moses the Ten Commandments.

This passage has been chosen because it tells us of a special food God gave Elijah. The passage connects with the gospel where Jesus tells us he is the bread that will strengthen us on our journey through life and into eternal life.

HOMILY – Last Sunday's gospel ended with Jesus telling us, "I am the bread of life; whoever comes to me will never hunger, and whoever believes in me will never thirst." This is one of the important "I am" statements in John's gospel. Throughout the gospel Jesus uses these statements to help us know who he is. Some of the other statements are: "I am the light of the world," "I am the vine, you are the branches," "I am the good shepherd," "I am the way the truth and the life." Then we have those two words standing alone, when Jesus came to his apostles walking on the water. They were frightened and Jesus said simply "I am. Do not be afraid." The Greek words are usually translated, "It is I" but the literal translation of "Ego eimi" is "I am." It recalls the name God gave to Moses, Yahweh, which is often translated, "I am who am." Unlike the rest of creation, God depends on no other being in order to be. God is being itself. Jesus said the same of himself, "ego eimi," "I am."

In last week's gospel the topic of manna came up. Manna is the bread that God gave his people in the desert as they made their way to the Promised Land. Jesus told them God was giving them something superior to this manna. God wanted to give them the true bread from heaven that gives life to the world. Then Jesus identified himself as that bread of life. He asked his listeners to believe in him and through their belief they would never be hungry or thirsty. In other words, all their needs would be satisfied. It was on that idea that last Sunday's gospel ended. Today's gospel continues, telling us the people murmured. They questioned how he could have come down from heaven. They knew his parents; they knew him when he was growing up. The murmuring is reminiscent of God's people in the desert on their way to the Promised Land. They didn't have faith God would care for them. It's this lack of faith the people show in today's gospel. They wouldn't believe that Jesus could do all these things he promised, that whoever eats the bread that God gives them, which is Jesus himself, that the way to eternal life would open for whoever believed in Jesus.

Having faith is the key to understanding today's gospel. In this section of John's sixth chapter, the focus in on Jesus who is given to us by the Father. He is the bread that nourishes us with eternal life. Our response to his coming to us is faith.

The passage ends with a line that will lead us next week into Jesus' teaching on the Eucharist. Belief in Jesus as the bread of life will naturally lead the believer to eat his body and drink his blood. This is where people's faith is stretched to the limit. I want to make a brief comment about this last line in today's gospel: "the bread that I will give is my flesh" St. John dedicates a large part of his gospel to the Last Supper, but he does not tell us about the institution of the Eucharist as the other gospels do. John says this about Jesus and the Eucharist: "the bread I will give is my flesh." Can you see how this is a perfect parallel to the words of consecration: when taking bread the priest says: "this is my body." "The bread I will give is my flesh."

Imagine going back in time 1000 years, when people traveled around by either walking or carriage or horseback. As we observe the people, the kings and rulers and the common people, most of whom were farmers, we observed the people's diet, which would have been very simple. We start telling people how they could improve their diet. We tell them about vitamins and cholesterol and protein and carbs and saturated and unsaturated fats and enzymes, etc. Surely they would think we were crazy. A lot of people thought Jesus was crazy when he told them he was the bread that would bring eternal life. Jesus is telling us today there is more to life than what we think we know or what we can figure out on our own. That's why he tells us to believe in him. Amen.

20th Sunday of Ordinary Time
August 19, 2012

INTRODUCTION – (Proverbs 9:1-6; Ephesians 5:15-20; John 6:51-58) The ninth chapter of the book of Proverbs speaks of two women – women who are symbols and not real: one is the symbol of wisdom and the other symbolizes foolishness. Thus they are named Lady Wisdom and Dame Folly. Each is pictured as the owner of an inn, and both are busy inviting people to stay at their guesthouse and partake of the meal they have prepared. Those who share the hospitality of Lady Wisdom are rewarded with joy and an abundance of life. Those who accept the invitation of Dame Folly are walking into a trap that will result in death. We hear in today's first reading the first part of chapter nine in Proverbs: the invitation of Lady Wisdom. The columns that are part of her house symbolize stability, while the number seven symbolizes perfection.

HOMILY – John begins the sixth chapter of his gospel with Jesus feeding over 5000 people with five loaves of bread and two fish. The people had seen his healing of the sick and now, after being fed, they began to think, "this is a good deal: free food. If he can do this for us, what more might he do?" So they decide to make him a king. The apostles would benefit greatly by his being a king as their importance in society would be significantly enhanced. He sends his apostles off by boat to Capernaum to get them away from the crowd, and he somehow slips away from the crowd himself. He rejoins his apostles in the middle of the night by walking on the water. When the crowd arrived back at Capernaum, they found Jesus there. Jesus told them their motives in looking for him were superficial. He had better things than a free meal to offer them. It was then Jesus identified himself as the bread of life, a food that would satisfy all their needs. Notice how at this point the focus shifts entirely onto the bread. We don't hear about the fish anymore.

Last week's gospel ended where this week's gospel begins: "the bread that I will give is my flesh." I pointed out how this statement parallels the words of institution at the Last Supper: Jesus took bread and said, "this is my body." This part of chapter six is explicitly Eucharistic. The people had difficulty believing what Jesus was telling them. Jesus did not back down to try to make it easier to accept. He didn't say, "the bread I will give will symbolize my body." He didn't say, "in spirit I will be hidden within the bread that I will give you." He said clearly, "the bread that I will give is my flesh," and he repeated the idea over and over with as much clarity as possible that his flesh and blood were food that would feed a person for eternal life. Because it is hard to believe, people have tried to explain away what Jesus is saying here. We will hear next week how many of his followers walked away from him after what he had said. Jesus did not call them back or say they misunderstood. Jesus knew they understood him perfectly.

Because they clearly understand the few simple words Jesus spoke, that's why others walk away today. (Everyone knows what "is" means.) I was thinking, "if I were pope I would have this gospel read at least once every two months." This is one of the biggest challenges Catholics have with their faith – believing Jesus is speaking seriously here. Jesus is very serious: "unless you eat the flesh of the Son of Man and drink his blood, you do not have life within you. For my flesh is true food and my blood is true drink." This eating and drinking is not a once in a while thing. It's like a good diet. We can't eat a healthy meal once in a while and expect it to do much for us. Jesus says, "whoever eats my flesh and drinks my blood remains in me and I in him." The body and blood of Christ maintains an ongoing relationship with Jesus.

The bread and the wine do not symbolize the body and blood of Christ. They are the body and blood of Christ. Because they are, they do symbolize a number of things, as for example, with his body and blood Christ keeps his divine life alive within us just as our daily food and drink keep us alive physically; that Christ loves us and wants to be close to us and wants us to stay close to him; the separate elements of body and blood represent our participation in Jesus' sacrificial death for us.

Our faith reminds us constantly that we live in two worlds. We live in the world we know and a world we don't know. The world we know encompasses all the things we can perceive through our senses and all the things we can conceive with our intellect. The world we do not know we will meet up with some day in all its glory. It is beyond our ability to know with our senses or our rational mind. We can only know it vaguely through analogy. We believe that Jesus came to reveal to us as much as we are capable of understanding what it will be like. "The one who comes from heaven testifies to what he has seen and heard," he tells Nicodemus. (Jn 3:31)

He has not only told us about the world that is to come for all of us, but he has given us a path to follow, the path of faith, hope and love for God and for others. He has given us a special help to strengthen us as we make this journey – his own flesh and blood. It's all spelled out clearly in today's gospel. The Eucharist is our connection with the world to come. "Just as the living Father sent me and I have life because of the Father, so also the one who feeds on me will have life because of me." (Jn. 6:57) What more can be said? Lots more, but we can't try to say it all today. Amen.

21st Sunday of Ordinary Time
August 26, 2012

INTRODUCTION – (Joshua 24:1-2a, 15-17, 18b; Eph 5:21-32; John 6:60-69) A man was robbing a bank and as he stood at the teller's window with a gun in his hands, his mask fell off. He quickly put it back on and turned to a man who was a bank customer and asked him, "Did you see my face?" The man said "yes, I saw you." And so the robber shot him. Then he turned to a couple who were standing nearby and said to the wife, "Did you see my face?" The wife said "No, I didn't see you. But my husband did!"

I wonder if that husband might have been the type of person who would give his wife a jab in the ribs when the lector reads today's second reading. Paul says "wives should be subordinate to their husbands." God did not make either husband or wife to be a dictator of the other. When you hear this reading, keep in mind the first sentence where Paul says to both husbands and wives: "Be subordinate to one another" You might notice that Paul is just as demanding (and maybe even more so) of husbands in this passage than he is of wives. Marriage involves mutual love and respect.

Shortly after God's people arrived in the Promised Land, Joshua, who became their leader after Moses died, gathered the people together to renew their covenant with Yahweh. They enthusiastically chose to commit themselves to follow God faithfully. History tells us later generations did not remain so enthusiastically faithful. In contrast with this commitment of fidelity, we hear in today's gospel that many of Jesus' disciples chose not to follow him after his teaching on the Eucharist. All the apostles stayed with him.

HOMILY – I'm sure it is somewhat uncomfortable to go to Mass with a lot of scaffolding between you and the altar. So I'll try not to make you suffer too long. Today we hear the conclusion of the sixth chapter of John's gospel. It began with Jesus feeding a huge crowd of people with five loaves of bread and two fish. The chapter moved on to a discussion about Jesus being the bread of life, then to Jesus' statement that we must eat his flesh and drink his blood if we wish to share in eternal life. We see in today's gospel the reaction to Jesus' teaching. People thought he was out of his mind and walked away from him. Jesus didn't try to explain what he had said so clearly and emphatically. The fact that Jesus let the people leave, knowing that they understood him literally, is a strong proof to me that this is the way he wants us to understand him when he says, "this is my body – this is the chalice of my blood."

As the people were walking away, Jesus simply asked his apostles if they wanted to leave him too. Peter, who often puts his foot in his mouth, came across this time with the right answer: "To whom shall we go? You have the words of eternal life. We have come to believe and are convinced that you are the Holy One of God."

Sometimes it's the only answer we can give to events in our lives. God's ways are often hidden from us. God tells us he loves us, he will always be with us, but we don't always experience that love or his presence. He tells us to love our enemies. To forgive those who have hurt us. To eat his body and drink his blood. Our faith challenges us to believe in what we cannot see or prove or perhaps not always feel or makes sense. In times of confusion or distress, we pray for help, we pray to understand. Our prayers seem to be unanswered. We seek counseling. Maybe it helps. But sometimes all we can end up doing is to say: "I believe. If Jesus said it, if Jesus said he loves us, he is with us, especially in the Eucharist, then I believe it because I believe in Jesus and he speaks the words of eternal life." That my friends is what faith is, pure and simple.

I promised I would not make you watch through the scaffolding too long, so I'll conclude my homily with that message. Amen.

22nd Sunday of Ordinary Time
September 2, 2012

INTRODUCTION – (Deut 4:1-2, 6-8; Jas 1:17-18, 21-22, 27; Mark 7:1-8, 14-15, 21-23) Today's first reading takes us back to the time of Moses right before God's people were to cross the Jordan and enter the Promised Land. Moses knew he would die before they crossed the Jordan. So he had some last words instructing and encouraging God's people before he parted from them. In essence he is telling God's people that God loves his people and he wants them to prosper. They will do so only if they keep God's laws. This passage fits well with our other two readings which teach us how important it is for our well-being in this world and our eternal happiness in the next to obey God.

HOMILY – It would take about four days to get from Jerusalem to Galilee, if you had to walk. Most people walked at the time of Jesus. So when we hear the beginning of today's gospel, that the Pharisees and some scribes from Jerusalem came together to observe Jesus, we know immediately that something is up, and these religious leaders were not interested in just saying "hello."

Right away they question Jesus as to why his disciples ate without washing their hands. Now washing hands before eating is a good practice. For the Pharisees, however, it was considered to be an offense against God. There was no law of God commanding it. It was part of an oral tradition that was presumed to have come down from Moses.

Jesus' response on the issue of hand washing went further than that issue alone. He attacked the very principle behind it, the principle that what we eat can make us unworthy to stand before God. It is part of Jewish law, as we all know, that Jews were not allowed to eat certain foods such as pork and shellfish. Jesus, on this occasion, made a pronouncement that dietary laws would no longer be binding. "Nothing that enters a person from outside can defile a person; but the things that come out from within are what defile," he said. This statement would have been enough to condemn Jesus as a lawbreaker and as a person who leads others to break God's laws. Jesus saw himself, however, as having the authority to interpret God's law and on various occasions, he didn't hesitate to do so. I might digress by noting that He also saw himself as having the authority to forgive sins, to heal the sick, to raise the dead, to cast out demons, to calm the stormy sea, to demand obedience to his word and to teach people about God and God's kingdom. People ask, did Jesus know he was God? He certainly acted as if he knew he was.

We must remember when we hear Jesus' statement, "Nothing that enters a person from outside can defile a person" Jesus is only talking about food. There were no magazines, books, movies or internet at Jesus time. Jesus is not talking about other things, such as pornography (which is a big industry today), that some people feed their minds and hearts with; he's not talking about recreational drugs that people feed themselves with. These things do not do them any good in their relationship with God or with others.

Our scriptures today are an encouragement to obey God. God's grace, which is a sharing in God's life and the path to eternal joy, calls us to a life of holiness. Moses, in the first reading, told God's people that God's law was a gift that would give evidence of wisdom and intelligence in those who followed God's law. James, in the second reading, is completely practical all through his letter, telling us that faith without works is dead. "We must be doers of the word and not hearers only." In today's gospel, Jesus gives a long list of sinful tendencies that are found in all human hearts, tendencies that we all struggle against in one form or another. These tendencies reveal why Jesus had to come to us, to help us to have love in our hearts: the love of God and love for each other. Amen.

23rd Sunday of Ordinary Time
September 9, 2012

INTRODUCTION – (Isaiah 35:4-7; Jas 2:1-5; Mark 7:31-37) The prophet Isaiah is speaking to God's people during their captivity in Babylon: "Be strong, fear not! Here is your God he comes to save you." God's salvation is expressed in terms of healing the blind and the deaf, the lame and the mute. The desert would come alive with rivers and springs and an abundance of life-giving water. The reading prepares us for the gospel where Jesus heals a man who was a deaf mute. Jesus' healing work was a work of compassion, but it also announced in a dramatic way God's saving presence among his people. In our own times of trial, we need to remind ourselves over and over again of these words of Isaiah: "Here is your God he comes to save you."

HOMILY – There was an old grandfather who was almost stone deaf. Without telling any of his family, he decided to go to a doctor and get a set of hearing aids that allowed him to hear almost perfectly. When grandfather want back to the doctor for his monthly checkup, the doctor said to him, I'll bet your family were really surprised and delighted to discover that you could now hear. He said, "I haven't told my family yet. I just sit around and listen. I've already changed my will three times." Well, it's a funny story, but as we age and lose some of our abilities or faculties it is not very humorous.

Jesus, in today's gospel, healed a man who was deaf and hardly able to speak. His need was very great in that he had to have friends bring him to Jesus. We see Isaiah's prophecy, which we heard in today's first reading, is beginning to be fulfilled. God is coming to save his people. We look forward to its completion in the resurrection on the last day. Jesus is creating a new world by "doing all things well."

We also see a message in this particular healing. Jesus wants us all to have our ears open to his word and to proclaim it. If we have trouble hearing what he wants to tell us, all we need to do is to ask him to open our ears for us. He will be only too glad to help.

When we were baptized, the priest or deacon touched

our ears and our mouth in imitation of Jesus and said: "The Lord Jesus made the deaf hear and the dumb speak. May he soon touch your ears to receive his word, and your mouth to proclaim his faith, to the praise and glory of God the Father." At the time of Jesus, spittle was viewed as a vehicle for supernatural power, and folk medicine (even advocated by "professional" physicians) at that time thought it had healing power. Especially for a holy person like Jesus, it was considered powerful. I wonder if we retain some of that concept even today when parents give their child a little kiss if the child skinned their knee or hurt themselves somewhere. Anyway, the minister of baptism doesn't use spittle any more – just his prayer and his touch.

It seems to have become more popular lately for people to openly declare that they are Catholics or Christians. It takes more than just going thru a baptismal ceremony to make that claim with any genuine sincerity. Having our ears opened and being called to proclaim our faith (whether by preaching it or living it) is an on-going process. That's why we encourage reading the Scriptures and why so much of the Mass is focused on God's word. May we all continue to have open ears and hearts to God's word, especially Jesus who is the Word of God. Amen.

24th Sunday in Ordinary Time
September 13, 2009

INTRODUCTION – (Isaiah 50:5-9; James 2:14-18; Mark 8:27-35) The book of the prophet Isaiah contains four poems commonly referred to as Servant Songs. They are mysterious passages because no one is sure whom they referred to originally. They describe one whom God had chosen from before birth – not only to serve God and to serve God's people in Israel, but to be a light to all nations. It's amazing how perfectly these Servant Songs, written over 500 years before Christ, describe Jesus. Today's passage describes how God's Servant would encounter resistance, persecution and martyrdom, and how God would stand by him during all his trials. We hear this same passage again on Palm Sunday and on Wednesday of Holy Week. It was chosen for today because we hear Jesus predict in today's gospel that suffering, death and resurrection are ahead for him.

HOMILY – Caesarea Philippi is one of the places I visited in the Holy Land 20 years ago. I still remember it well. It is in northern Galilee near where the Jordan river begins. The area in not dry like most of Israel, but it is lush with much vegetation and water. There is a shrine there that was dedicated to the Greek god, Pan. The shrine is carved into a high cliff, along with a number of other niches, which held statues of Greek and Roman gods and goddesses. It was in this setting that Jesus asked his disciples, "Who do people say I am?" Then he asked, "Who do you say I am?" Here is the Son of God asking, "We see ourselves surrounded by all these gods and goddesses. Who do you say that I am?" Peter said, "You are the Christ, i.e., you are the Messiah, the long awaited savior." The word Messiah is from the Hebrew, which designated one who was anointed, that is: a king or a priest. The Greek word for Messiah is Christos. Jesus told them not to tell anyone about him; Jesus may have had several reasons why he didn't want them to tell others about him, but one reason is obvious from the gospels: Peter could recognize Jesus as Messiah, but he really had only a limited idea of what Messiah meant. Jesus instructed them that it meant Jesus would have to suffer if he were going to save the people – an idea Peter rejected and for which Jesus severely reprimanded him.

It is this problem of suffering that is precisely where a lot of people lose faith in God or lose faith in Christ. We see so much suffering around us and we ask, "Why doesn't God put a stop to all this suffering?" or "Why does Christ allow this or that tragedy to happen?" I was asking myself this question Friday while thinking of what happened on 9/11/2001. Like Peter we want to say: "This cannot be."

Most of us have a favorite way of picturing Jesus: as Savior, or an understanding friend, or a merciful and forgiving person, a great teacher, a powerful healer, a good shepherd, as the Sacred Heart, an advocate for the poor, an eternal king, the Son of God, a great storyteller. But to think of him in his sufferings and as one who tells us if we want to follow him we might have to suffer too – that's not an image many people like to dwell on. I know from my own experience that when I am suffering, it is very comforting to think of how Jesus suffered. Other than Lent, I don't believe most people reflect much on Christ as our suffering savior. The gospels, especially today's gospel, tells us that's a big part of who Jesus is and that's how he saved us all.

It's so much a part of who he is it's the principal way he asked us to remember him. He gave us his body to eat – his body which he gave for us, and his blood to drink – his blood which he shed for us; and he said "do this in remembrance of me." I wonder if this is perhaps the reason why people so easily excuse themselves from Mass, because, like Peter, they still have to learn about the mystery and the power of the cross. Like Peter most of us want a Messiah (a Christ) who will take away our problems – not one who has to suffer and who tells us to take up our cross if we wish to follow him.

Let me conclude with two points. First of all, I want to say something about suffering. Simply because we are human, we're going to face suffering of one kind or another. Do not think following Christ will make your crosses in life any heavier, on the contrary it will make them lighter and easier to bear. Peter hadn't come to that understanding yet in today's gospel, but eventually he did.

The final point is that when Jesus said "whoever wishes to save his life will lose it and whoever loses his life for my sake will save it," does not mean we all have to be martyrs if we want to get to heaven. What Jesus said about losing one's life was literally true in many cases in the early Church when there were persecutions, and it is literally true in some parts of the world today. We must be willing to hold on to our faith even in the face of death. But for people in 21st century in countries where there is religious freedom, we need to understand that losing our life for Christ means basically losing the selfish, proud, negative, unholy side of ourselves so that we can be the kind of person who pleases God. In this we will be saved.

In the question "who do you say that I am?" it's not enough just to be able to give the right answer. The gospels show us that coming to know Jesus is an on-going process throughout our lives. It's a matter of getting to know him better and not trying to make him into who we want him to be. Amen.

Feast of the Holy Cross
September 14, 2008

INTRODUCTION – (Numbers 21:4b-9; Philippians 2:6-11; John 3:13-17) Our first reading takes us back over a thousand years before Christ, to the time when Moses was leading God's people from slavery in Egypt to the freedom of the Promised Land. The trip through the desert was extremely difficult and at times the people complained bitterly. One of their difficulties was an encounter with a nest of poisonous serpents whose bite brought intense suffering and burning pain and then death. The serpents were called saraph serpents, for saraph means "fiery." The people saw this as punishment for their complaining. But God gave them a way to be healed from the serpent's bite. The remedy might remind us of the symbol often used today as an icon of the medical profession. In today's gospel, Jesus compares this event to his crucifixion.

HOMILY – During Holy Week we focus on the sufferings of Christ crucified. Today our focus is more on the glory and victory of the cross. In Jesus' day the cross was an instrument of torture, brutality and shame. The Romans reserved it for the worst criminals and enemies of the Roman Empire. If a criminal was a Roman citizen, he or she was exempt from crucifixion because it was such a terrible way to die. Roman citizens were simply beheaded. But Jesus has turned the cross into a symbol of victory, a symbol of hope, a symbol of sacrifice and infinite love. St. Paul tells us in Galatians (2:20) "I live by faith in the Son of God who has loved me and given himself up for me."

Over and over the Scriptures tell us through the cross Jesus saved us, but early Christian art seldom pictured the cross. They didn't need to. Father Foley in Saint of the Day said: "It stood outside too many city walls, decorated only with decaying corpses, as a threat to anyone who defied Rome's authority." Included in this group of those who defied Rome's authority were the Christians who would not worship pagan gods, but only the Father, the Lord Jesus and the Spirit. The emperor Constantine who made Christianity legal in 313 also eliminated crucifixion as a form of capital punishment. Once the Roman Empire actually ceased crucifying people, then images of the cross appeared in Christian art. These first images of the cross did not include an image of the suffering Christ, but they were crosses decorated with jewels and precious metals. Incidentally it was a vision of the cross that led to the conversion of Constantine. He was assured in the vision that in the sign of the cross he would conquer Maxentius, a rival to the throne, and he would become emperor of Rome.

Once Constantine gained control of the Roman Empire, he went to the Holy Land with his mother, St. Helen, to discover the places where Jesus lived and died. Constantine and his mother had churches built in Bethlehem and the Mount of Olives but the most famous church he built is the Church of the Holy Sepulcher, built over the hill of Calvary and the tomb of Jesus. It was in the process of building the Church of the Holy Sepulcher that Jesus' cross was found. How did they know it was Jesus' cross? Legend has it that the men working on this project found three crosses and they didn't know which one was Jesus' cross. They touched each of the crosses to a woman who was dying and when she was touched with the third cross, she was instantly healed. Today's feast of the Holy Cross goes back to that time, around the year 320 AD. It celebrates the finding of the true cross and the dedication of the Basilica of the Holy Sepulcher. So that's why this feast is celebrated in the middle of September and not during Lent as we might expect.

Today's gospel is sometimes called the gospel in miniature. These few verses express the essence of the entire gospel: God's offer of eternal life through the sacrifice of Christ, a sacrifice offered out of love for us. God so loved the world, God so loved you and me that he gave us the greatest gift, the gift of his son, so we would know the greatest blessing: eternal happiness with him. Today we approach the cross not with sorrow but with joy, not as a symbol of death but of life, not as a sign of defeat but of victory, not as a cause for fear but of hope, not as an instrument of cruelty and hatred but of eternal love. On a practical level, I know somehow it was inevitable if Jesus were to be true to his mission. If he had run away from it, he would not have risen and his message would have soon been forgotten. Today Christians make up one third of the world's population. If Jesus had abandoned his mission to change the world through love, perhaps some obscure history book might have had a sentence or two about this person who did a lot of healing and was a good preacher, but for the most part his ministry would be forgotten. This is just a superficial explanation of the mystery of the cross. There is much more to this mystery, but each of us has to discover it for ourselves. To come to a deeper understanding takes lots of prayer – and that's what the Mass does for us each week, it reminds us of God's love and the hope and joy and freedom and peace and salvation it gives us. Amen.

25th Sunday in Ordinary Time
September 20, 2009

INTRODUCTION – (Wisdom 2:12, 17-20; James 3:16-4:3; Mark 9:30-37) In 333 BC, Alexander the Great conquered everything between Egypt and India. For a little over 250 years, the Greeks controlled all of the Middle East including the Holy Land. The Greek rulers decided all nations under their rule should accept Greek culture and religion. The Jews were being forced to give up their belief in Yahweh, the one God they had served (not always faithfully) for 1500 years. Those who did not submit were persecuted or killed. Some of the Jews converted to Greek ways and pagan worship and some stayed faithful to Yahweh. The Jews who turned to paganism speak in today's first reading from the Book of Wisdom. They plot against the faithful Jew, sarcastically refer to him or her as "the just one" and ridicule traditional faith in God. The first reading connects with the gospel in that Jesus who is truly the "just one" predicts the suffering he will have to face for remaining faithful to God's work.

HOMILY – The first thing that strikes me about today's gospel is the stark contrast between Jesus and his disciples. Jesus was trying to prepare them for the sufferings he would endure (this was the second time he raised the topic) and they were preoccupied with which of them was the greatest. They just did not understand what Jesus was trying to tell them, and St. Mark tells us, "they were afraid to question him."

Jesus had a lot of big egos in his group. With that attitude they wouldn't make very good disciples, so he had to have a little talk with them. It is easy to imagine that as Jesus is talking with them, there a few children were close by. Jesus motioned to one child to come to him and, putting his arms around the child, Jesus demonstrated the kind of attitude he expected of his followers. In that society children were greatly loved, but they had no social status. They depended totally on the goodwill of their elders. If his disciples were to learn from Jesus and imitate him, they would not be worried about who would be most important in the kingdom; they would become more like Jesus in their thinking. Jesus' attitude was that of service. "If anyone wishes to be first, he shall be the last of all and the servant of all." Jesus himself came "not to be served but to serve" as he would tell them later. (Mk 10:45)

Jesus is not asking us to adopt the attitude that we are not worth anything or that we have no importance. When Jesus said we should love our neighbor as ourselves, he implies that we should love ourselves – otherwise we won't be very good at loving anyone else. As a matter of fact, each of us is of infinite worth because Jesus shed his blood for us, so much does he love us. If all we do is put ourselves down, this will not make us holy, it will just make us depressed. The Christian spirit is a spirit of joy, not depression. We could say that what Jesus was trying to impress on his disciples was not that they think less of themselves, rather that they think of themselves less. This is an attitude that will help us be more sensitive to the needs of others.

In writing this, I was thinking of Jesus and his service to us. His service to us begins, of course, with creation – with loving us and willing us into being. As we say in the creed: "through him all things were made." Then he, the infinite Son of God, took on our human nature in the womb of Mary. As Paul said, he emptied himself and took on the form of a slave. He spent his public ministry teaching, healing, casting out demons and accepting rejection and abuse for his work of service. He met with hostility from the powers that be and even a gruesome death rather than abandon his work of service. His work of service continues to this day by his presence with us, especially his presence in the Eucharist as he gives us his body and his blood to be our food and source of eternal life.

You've probably all heard this story before about the man who died and went to heaven. He was amazed when he got there to find people he never expected to find. He commented to God: "I never expected to find some of these people here and, by the way, why is everyone so quiet?" God said, "they didn't expect to see you here." Most of us will probably be greatly surprised when we get to heaven and see who is there and who enjoys a more exalted position. We may see the local schoolteacher or fireman or cleaning lady or secretary enjoying a higher rank and greater happiness than kings or generals or millionaires or famous entertainers.

We praise and thank God for all he has done for us. Let us pray we might learn from his example of generous kindness and service to us. Amen.

26th Sunday in Ordinary Time
September 27, 2009

HOMILY – (Nm 11:25-29; Jas 5:1-6; Mark 9:38-43, 45, 47-48) Calvin Coolidge was a man of few words. When he returned from church one Sunday morning his wife asked him what the preacher talked about. Wilson answered "sin." When she asked him what he said about it, he answered "he was agin' it." Dr. Karl Menninger, the world famous psychiatrist who died just a few years ago at the age of 97, wrote a book entitled *Whatever became of sin?* His book begins with a story about a man on a busy street corner in downtown Chicago about 20 years ago. The man was tall, thin, and looked grim and solemn as he watched people walk by. Occasionally he would point a finger at a person coming toward him and say the one word: "guilty." Probably many people who had the finger pointed at them wondered "How does he know?"

That was 20 years ago. If someone were to do something like today I wonder how many would walk away not asking themselves "How does he know?" but asking themselves "I wonder what he means by that?" The thesis of Dr. Menninger's book is that society has lost its sense of sin. In his book *Whatever became of sin?*, Dr. Menninger is not trying to tell us that sin has gone out of existence, but to the contrary, he is telling us it has become a greater problem in society simply because many today are indifferent to the reality of sin. Yet that is what our readings are about today. Sin is what St. James is speaking of when he talks about social injustice and lack of concern for those in need. Sin is what our Lord is talking about too, when he tells us to cut off our hand, our foot, or tear out our eye if it is going to lead us from God and into damnation. This is a metaphor of course. Our Lord doesn't really intend us to go and mutilate ourselves in this way because sin does not find its origin in our hands or feet but in our mind and heart. Sin is a decision to do something God has forbidden or not to do something God has commanded.

In telling us this Jesus is sharing a vision with us that he can see more clearly than any of us can. His vision is that if we want lasting happiness we must hold our relationship with God as more precious than anything else we possess. Especially he emphasizes this with regard to leading little children away from God, not teaching them right, giving them bad example or even abusing them. Think for a moment, this is the gentle, merciful, loving Jesus who is speaking to us when he tells us it would be better for someone to have a great stone tied around their neck and be dropped into the sea rather than lead astray one of God's little ones. Some people want to think Jesus is soft on sin. Truly Jesus is forgiving, but Jesus does not consider sin to be trivial.

Adam and Eve's story in the beginning of the bible is a perfect illustrations of the destructive nature of sin. Adam and Eve were created in a state of happiness, living in peace and harmony with God, with each other and with nature. But they listened to the tempter who told them God gave them rules in order to keep them from greater fulfillment and happiness. To make a long story short, they chose not to trust God and to pursue the happiness they thought God was hiding from them. This failure to trust led to disobedience, and this sin brought to an end the peace and harmony they enjoyed. They could not face God, nor could they face each other. Their innocence was gone. They were embarrassed by their nakedness. Adam tried to blame Eve for his sin while she blamed the serpent. They were even out of harmony with nature. God told them it would only be by sweat and hard work that they would obtain the food they needed. The story tells us sin, any sin, but especially serious sin, harms our relationships with God, with one another and with all of creation.

In scripture, the term for sin that is most often used is a word that means "missing the mark." It is as if someone is shooting an arrow or throwing a ball and their aim is off. Our aim in life, our purpose and our greatest happiness in life will be when all our relationships are perfect, when we are totally one with God, one within our own person (that is, being integrated, not at war within ourselves) and one with each other. This perfect state will be heaven. When we sin, we are missing our real goal in life. We are taking a path that will lead us nowhere near our goal. Theologians have categorized seven different paths we human beings have a tendency to travel that lead us away from our goal. If you remember your catechism, you will recognize them as the seven capital sins: pride, covetousness, lust, anger, gluttony, envy and laziness, especially laziness in our spiritual lives.

Jesus is telling us sin is nothing to play with. It can get a hold on us and not let go easily. There is a story told about a lamb that wandered out onto a frozen section of the Niagara River. The ice broke loose where the lamb was standing, leaving the lamb stranded. Eventually the poor little animal froze to death. An eagle saw the animal and started to make a delicious feast of this fresh frozen lamb. The eagle didn't have to worry that the piece of ice was floating toward the falls. After all, the eagle had powerful wings and could easily fly away. But when the ice floe came to the falls, the eagle discovered that its claws had become frozen in the ice and the eagle went cascading down the falls with the lamb. When we flirt with sin, we tell ourselves we can quit anytime, but often we can't.

When I mentioned to one of our parishioners that I was going to talk about sin, she said "Oh…. I wonder what time St. Ignatius is having Mass this weekend." People devour tabloids and talk shows that reveal the deviant or immoral behavior of others, especially celebrities, but for these same people to come to church and have to listen to a sermon on sin is another story. Such a sermon is almost as popular as a sermon on money. If we have sinned, which we all have, this sermon is not intended to make everyone feel guilty. We must remember when God forgives us he also totally forgets. The purpose of this sermon is to call to repentance those who need to repent as well as to remind all of us that sin is a reality and ignoring it will give it a greater hold on us. If we ignore the reality of sin we will also be ignoring the words of Jesus, the gentle Jesus, who tells us in a most emphatic way that it is something we have to take seriously, because it can destroy for us the eternal happiness he wants for us.

27th Sunday of Ordinary Time
October 7, 2012

HOMILY – (Genesis 2:18-24; Hebrews 2:9-11; Mark 10:2-12) A comedian (I think it was Red Skelton) talking about his marriage once said, our marriage greatly improved once we got separate bedrooms. Hers is in New York and mine is in Miami. Whether a person is married or whether a person lives a single life, there will be challenges. Jesus talks to us today about marriage and some of its challenges. As our gospel begins, some Pharisees ask him if it were lawful for a husband to divorce his wife. The gospel tells us they asked this question as a test. We will see in a moment what they were up to. Jesus saw it right away.

Jewish society was a male dominated society, and the issue in today's gospel is all about a man divorcing his wife. In the Jewish culture, a woman could not divorce her husband. The Pharisees' question is if divorce is lawful. Most Jews thought it was lawful since Moses, in Deuteronomy, seems to have permitted a husband to divorce his wife. If you read the actual passage in Deuteronomy (Deut. 24:1ff), you would see that Moses never declared divorce was lawful. The fact is that nowhere in the Old Testament is divorce said to be lawful. The prophet Malachi says clearly God hates divorce (Malachi 2:16). A better understanding of Moses' attitude toward divorce would be that he overlooked it in view of the people's hardness of heart – whatever that might have meant. He did make certain rules about divorce if it occurred. By the time of Jesus, however, divorce among the Jews was considered lawful although it was probably not all that frequent. But there is something more behind the Pharisee's question whether divorce was lawful. If we look at Matthew's gospel, the question the Pharisees ask is whether it is lawful to divorce one's wife for any cause? That was the real issue and that's where there was a lot of controversy. Some rabbis allowed divorce only for the most serious reason while others allowed divorce if the wife spoiled a dinner or if the man found himself attracted to someone else.

In answering the Pharisee's question, Jesus showed himself, as he often did, as having the authority to interpret God's law. He brushed aside all their questions about whether it was lawful or unlawful, or under what circumstances it was lawful or unlawful. He said there should be no divorce at all. Then Jesus referred to the story of creation (our first reading) for Scriptural proof that it was God's intention that when God made man and woman they became one flesh and no human being had the power to separate them. Practically speaking, there are situations where people need to separate, where their relationship is toxic or unmanageable or even possibly lethal. Even Jesus knew that could happen, but he adds to his teaching that should it happen the divorced person is to remain unmarried: "whoever divorces his wife and marries another commits adultery against her." Mark adds, and if the wife "divorces her husband and marries another, she commits adultery." This added thought applied Jesus' teachings to those

Gentiles who would be converting to Jesus, for, even though Jewish women could not sue for divorce, Gentile women were, by Roman law, allowed to sue for divorce.

Jesus has given us his teaching on marriage and divorce. That is important in view of the common attitude today that marriage is for many people whatever they want it to be; that it is a personal arrangement between two people who can make it or break it whenever they choose. The solemn commitment "for better or for worse until death" has little meaning for many people today. That's why Jesus' teaching is difficult for today's world. Yet if we believe in Jesus as God's spokesperson, then his teachings (and not the attitude that dominates our culture) must guide our thinking about marriage.

This teaching of Jesus is in Matthew, Luke and St. Paul. Matthew makes an exception to Jesus' sanction of divorce and remarriage when he quotes Jesus as saying: "whoever divorces his wife, except for immorality, and marries another, commits adultery." (Mt. 19:9) The phrase "except for immorality" has been greatly debated. The Greek word used here, which is translated immorality, is πορνεύω (porneuó). The English word pornographic comes from this word. In the Greek dictionary, it means "various kinds of unsanctioned sexual intercourse." On the basis of this exception, many people would like to believe that if their spouse is unfaithful, divorce and remarriage is permitted. This is not the Catholic understanding of Matthew. Our understanding of this passage is that the exception Matthew makes refers to marriages that were already unlawful such as marriages between close relatives. Hence Matthew's exception is not an exception to Jesus' general prohibition of divorce and remarriage; rather Matthew is saying that Jesus' teaching does not apply to relationships that are already forbidden by God's law.

The Catholic Church has always tried to be loyal to Jesus' teaching in its policies on marriage and it's not always a popular stand. Many people, whose first marriage failed, have sought and received an annulment from the Church and have been able to be married in the Church a second time. When the Church grants an annulment, it is not granting a divorce. An annulment simply states that a particular marriage, even if it were valid civilly, did not meet the standards for validity required by the Church and, therefore, the couple are not bound to one another in God's eyes. But even if a person could not get an annulment, the Church does not encourage the person to break up with a second spouse if they have one but to continue to come to Mass and to live a good Christian life to the best of their abilities. We see how pastorally Jesus treated the woman he met at the Samaritan well who had been married to five husbands (John 4:17-18).

There is so much that could be said about this topic. If we had another half hour (which we don't have) we could comment on the serious effects divorce has on society and on children who are the product of a broken marriage. Three hundred years before Christ, the philosopher Aristotle said, "divorce is to family life what civil war is to the state." Since the matter of divorce is often painful, it is helpful to remember that Jesus' deep intent was not to cause pain but to set out a clear and high ideal of human relations, a vision of marriage as a covenant of personal love between spouses which reflects the covenant relationship of God and his people. Unfortunately, this vision does not always fit the vagaries of the human heart. (Jer. 17:9)" *The New Jerome Biblical Commentary*, pg 643, #32

28th Sunday Ordinary Time
October 14, 2012

HOMILY – (Wisdom 7:7-11; Heb 4:12-13; Mark 10:17-30) Attitudes toward wealth were ambiguous in the ancient world as well as in Jewish literature. Deuteronomy and some of the Wisdom writings tell us those who obey God's commandments will be rewarded with prosperity. On the other hand, the prophets condemned those who were wealthy for they often took advantage of the poor and had lavish lifestyles without giving consideration to those who were needy. (Jesus' parable of the rich man and Lazarus reflects this attitude.) Our first reading reminds us that there are more precious things in life than having big stashes of wealth. The author of the Book of Wisdom prayed for prudence and the spirit of Wisdom and stated all gold, in view of her (Wisdom), is a little sand, and before her, silver is to be accounted mire (swampy ground or mud). This is very similar to Plato's teaching in the Republic that true riches come with a good and prudent life rather than from the counterfeit treasures of gold.

Perhaps the apostles were thinking of the idea in Deuteronomy that those who obey God's commandments will be rewarded with prosperity. They were surprised to hear Jesus say, "how hard it will be for those who have wealth to enter the kingdom of God." Then Jesus goes on to say that entering the kingdom is not easy for any of us: "Children, how hard it is to enter the kingdom of God." No one knows of any gate in Jerusalem called the "eye of the needle." Jesus' example of a camel getting through the eye of a needle was a graphic way of saying it's not possible. It's only possible with God's grace: "For human beings it is impossible, but not for God. All things are possible for God."

Jesus' response after the rich young man left was in disappointed surprise. He saw that the rich man, whom Jesus saw with love, would prefer worldly wealth to the riches of the kingdom of God. Sometimes those who have some wealth, even a modest amount, feel they are being condemned when they hear today's gospel. Let's realize first of all, practically speaking, the early missionaries, such as St. Paul, would have had great difficulty in founding Churches in various cities and towns without the help of those who were wealthy. The early Churches had to gather somewhere to hear God's word and to celebrate the Eucharist and that was usually at the home of someone of means whose place was large enough to accommodate everyone. Remember church buildings did not exist until the 4th century.

I want to remind you of two other places where Jesus expresses a negative view, or at least a cautious view, of wealth. Jesus said: "where your treasure is there will your heart be." (Mt. 6:21). In that sense, any of us could be led astray by wealth, however much we may have or not have, if we lose our focus on God's kingdom. The other place is where Jesus tells the story of the sower and the seed. Remember the seed that fell among the weeds and as it tried to grow it got choked out. Jesus compared this to those "who hear the word, but the cares of the world, and the lure of wealth, and the desire for other things come in and choke the word and it yields nothing." (Mk.4:19) In that sense, even the poorest among us can be so absorbed by activities and distractions, TV and cell phones and magazines and music and sports and computers, etc., we make no time to pray or come to Church or live as Christ has taught us. That's my homily on the gospel. God has blessed us in many ways. Let us not forget where it comes from.

I want to say a few things personally. The other day I

was with a few people and the topic of birthday's came up. I mentioned I was turning 75 on Sunday. One person commented "you're doing pretty good for 75;" and she added with great surprise, "you still drive!" For a split second I worried that maybe I should turn in my car keys. Canon Law requires pastors to write a letter of resignation to the Archbishop when they turn 75. Of course I did, but I added that I would be willing to continue serving here if he wished. Part of the process the Archdiocese has when a pastor turns 75 is for Bishop Binzer to meet with the Parish Pastoral Council, which he did here last week. Next week the Priests' Personnel Board meets and they will make a recommendation to the Archbishop. I feel very sure the Archbishop and the Personnel Board will decide that I stay here.

Other than not having as much energy as I used to, and other than my knees, I would feel in every other way as if I were 20 years younger. My knees keep reminding me though that I'm 75. Several people have asked me if I have Parkinson's when they see my right hand shake. It doesn't always bother me, but I do not have Parkinson's. The doctor said it is just a benign tremor that people sometimes experience only with their right hand. When I go out to eat sometimes, it is embarrassing, and it makes it hard to write legibly, but I could have worse problems. In my early years as a priest I used to enjoy painting and thought I could do a lot more painting when I retired. That's out of the question now (and maybe retirement will be too). I remind myself that Thomas Jefferson started the University of Virginia, secured its location, designed its buildings, planned its curriculum and became its first rector at the age of 76.

I like being here; I like doing what I'm doing most of the time (except when I have three weeks' worth of work that has to be completed in three days). St. Boniface has been good to me and I've tried to return the favor. I'm grateful for all the support I have always been given and the response of our parishioners whenever I've asked for your help. So I'll just say thank you and hope you will keep me in your prayers as I enter into what is laughingly referred to as the "Golden Years." Peace to every one of you.

29th Sunday Ordinary Time
October 21, 2012

INTRODUCTION – (Isaiah 53:10-11; Heb 4:14-16; Mk 10:35-45) Today our first reading is a portion of Isaiah's fourth Servant Song. Isaiah tells us God's servant was a mysterious person or persons whose faithfulness and suffering would bring redemption to many people. The four Servant Songs of Isaiah were written 500 years before Christ. This passage was chosen because it corresponds with Jesus' revelation in today's gospel to his apostles that he came to serve and to give his life as a ransom for many. The entire fourth Servant Song is part of the Good Friday service every year.

HOMILY – Jesus told James and John in today's gospel: "you do not know what you are asking." Indeed they did not. James and John, along with all the Apostles, had no idea what the future held for any of them. Peter had recently confessed that Jesus was the Christ, the Messiah which means the anointed one. They expected Jesus would soon be the glorified ruler of God's people. The Romans, who governed all the area around the Mediterranean, would no longer control Israel. The Apostles figured they would be Jesus' chief generals, sharing in his glory. They saw themselves lifted high, enjoying honor, prestige, importance and authority.

It's not a flattering picture of James and John or of the other Apostles who were angry at James and John for this display of selfish ambition. St. Matthew softened this negative picture of James and John by telling us in his gospel that the mother of James and John came forward to ask this special favor for her sons. It is possible that she was involved in one way or another in trying to get her sons raised in importance and rank above the rest.

Just moments before James and John approached Jesus with their bold request, Jesus had told them for the third time that he "will be turned over to the chief priests and the scribes, and they will condemn him to death and turn him over to the Gentiles and they will mock him and spit on him and scourge him and kill him; and after three days he will arise." It's a wonder Jesus didn't just pull his hair out or laugh right in their faces when James and John came to him asking him to do for them whatever they wanted. But that was not Jesus' style. He knew the Apostles still had a lot to learn. He patiently discussed their request with them and in the process of giving them an answer, he was able to teach them further. They still didn't understand, but Jesus planted the idea in their mind about what was important in God's kingdom. It is service done in love, not an erotic kind of love, but a kind of love that cares and that often requires sacrifice. Jesus' love led him to be faithful to his mission of preaching, teaching, healing, and casting out demons – a mission that brought him into conflict with the religious leaders and which eventually cost him his life. God was glorified in Jesus' loving service to God's people and God's power overcame those who plotted against Jesus and who thought they destroyed him. God's power even overcame the power of death by rising to new life, a life Jesus has promised to share with those who follow his way, his way of obedience to the Father and of loving service to others.

Eventually the Apostles would learn the important message Jesus taught: "Whoever wishes to be great among you will be your servant;" for as long as they stayed near Jesus they would have the example of the One who came "to serve and to give his life as a ransom for many." Jesus gave us the Eucharist to help us celebrate and remember that great love and to be able to share in its saving and life-giving power. Amen.

30th Sunday of Ordinary Time
October 28, 2012

HOMILY – (Jeremiah 31:7-9; Heb 5:1-6; Mark 10:46-52) In today's gospel Bartimaeus, the blind beggar, could see Jesus more clearly than everyone who had physical sight. He could see beyond what others could see with their eyes as he called out to Jesus: "Son of David, Jesus, have mercy on me." There is a lot packed into those few words. "Son of David" was a royal title referring to a descendant of the great king David, one who would be anointed by God to be king and savior of God's people. The Greek word for "the anointed one" is "Christos" or in English, "Christ." Bartimaeus was not the first person to recognize Jesus as the Son of David or as the Christ. Peter did at Caesarea Philippi when Jesus asked the Apostles: "who do you say that I am." The crowd who welcomed Jesus into Jerusalem had also recognized Jesus as Son of David. When Jesus entered Jerusalem, the crowd called out as he came riding in on a donkey: "Hosanna to the Son of David. Hosanna means, "Save, please!" I say all this so you know that Bartimaeus was not the only person who recognized Jesus as the royal Messiah and who was willing to address him as Son of

David. Bartimaeus had more than just a generic faith that Jesus came to save everyone; he knew the saving power of the Son of David could and would save him. His faith was deeply personal. He did not let himself be discouraged by those who told him to be quiet when he called out to Jesus. Rather he only got louder when people tried to silence him: "Son of David, have mercy (or pity) on me." I might mention in the original Greek "have mercy" is ἐλεέω (eleeó). It is a Greek word that many of us remember from the old Latin Mass: Kyrie, eleison. (Kyrie means Lord, by the way.) Like Bartimaeus, we begin our Mass asking God to have mercy or pity on us. This is not just a plea for forgiveness of sins. The kyrie eleison is a plea for God or Jesus to help us in any way we need his help. As we cry Kyrie eleison, (Lord, have mercy!) he invites us, as he invited Bartimaeus, to tell him: "what do you want me to do for you?" That's why we pause for a moment before the opening prayer – to mention in our hearts our special intentions.

On Monday afternoon I started reflecting on today's gospel about Jesus healing blindness. Later that evening I listened to the debates on TV. I came away from the debates thinking this is one area where we all need a clear vision to see beyond all the hoopla and spin that comes out of politics so we can cast our vote for a leader who will lead our country with respect for the values of life, liberty and the pursuit of happiness. Each of us must pray for guidance on whom that leader might be.

Certain issues that are both political and moral may be and should be addressed in Church, as for example: abortion, but we are not supposed to speak in support of candidates or political parties, so don't worry, I'm not going to get political. As the week progressed and as I continued to reflect on today's gospel, I thought that the main forms of blindness we humans have to deal with are our illusions, and they are many. Let me illustrate what I mean by illusion. There was a cartoon in Reader's Digest (*Laughter, the Best Medicine*, pg 152) displaying four people sunbathing on a Florida beach: there was a lady in her late 60's I would guess, engaged in conversation with a lady friend next to her. The husband of the first lady was near his wife, but not sunbathing. He was standing up, a huge man, especially large around the middle, holding up his arms as if to show his muscles, with a big grin on his face. This gesture was a way of trying to show off in front of a young, beautiful woman with a skimpy bathing suit who happened to be walking by at that moment, and who was totally unimpressed by his overly massive abdomen. His wife, the lady in her 60's, was saying to her friend: "my son's into extreme sports, my daughter's into extreme makeover, and my husband's into extreme denial." Denial and illusion are two sides of the same coin. We deny what really is because we have the illusion that reality is something else. Other examples: a person might imagine that they are the most wonderful human being who has ever walked the face of the earth, (and you may have known such people) or, conversely a person might think that he or she is the most miserable person who ever lived. A person might think themselves to be another Einstein or they might be always putting themselves down as just a big jerk. I have met both kinds. Probably the greatest illusion many people have is thinking they don't need God except maybe once a week. Or for some, maybe not even that often. For these people, God is just a word they use if they get angry or if they hurt themselves – although they have him tucked away in a closet somewhere just in case they get some really serious problem. The reality is we need God to support us at every moment of our lives. We are not as "in charge" as we would like to believe we are. That is reality.

Bartimaeus had a depth of inner vision in Jesus as his Messiah and Savior. He wasn't going to abandon his plea for help even when everyone else around him told him to "forget it." After Jesus healed him, Jesus told him to "go your way." Bartimaeus decided to make his "way" the way of Jesus and Mark tells us Bartimaeus followed Jesus "on the way," the way that led to Jerusalem and suffering, death and resurrection. In this miracle story, St. Mark, no doubt, is encouraging his hearers (and us) to choose Jesus as our leader and to follow his way – the way that leads to life.

All Saints
November 1, 2009

INTRODUCTION – (Rev. 7:2-4, 9-14; 1 John 3:1-3; Mt. 5:1-12a) Our first reading is from the book of Revelation. The section just preceding today's passage describes the end of the world. The sun will become dark and the moon will become red as blood and there will be a great earthquake all over the earth. People will try to hide from all these terrible things and they will ask: "Who can survive?" Today's reading is the answer to that question – those will survive who have followed Christ faithfully. The number 144,000 is a symbolic number, symbolizing perfection. Notice after it refers to the 144,000 it speaks of those who are saved as such a large crowd that no one can count them.

HOMILY – I am part of our parish book club and a few months ago Thomas Merton's *Seven Storey Mountain* was chosen as the book we would read. I totally loved the book and since then have read three other books about or by Thomas Merton and have begun reading a few others. To say the least, I was greatly impressed by him. There is a passage from *Seven Storey Mountain* I would like to read to you. At this point in Merton's life he was a new Catholic, not yet six months away from having been baptized. He is with his friend Robert Lax. Let me read it in Merton's own words.

They were walking down Sixth Avenue one evening when Lax asked Merton: "What do you want to be, anyway?" In Merton's own words: I could not say, "I want to be Thomas Merton the well-known writer of all those book reviews in the back pages of the Times Book Review," or " Thomas Merton the assistant instructor of Freshman-English at the New Life Social Institute for Progress and Culture," so I put the thing on the spiritual plane, where I knew it belonged and said: "I don't know; I guess what I want is to be a good Catholic." "What do you mean, you want to be a good Catholic?" The explanation I gave was lame enough, and expressed my confusion, and betrayed how little I had really thought about it at all. Lax did not accept it. "What you should say" – he told me – "what you should say is that you want to be a saint." A saint! The thought struck me as a little weird. I said: "how do you expect me to become a saint?" "By wanting to," said Lax, simply. "I can't be a saint," I said, "I can't be a saint." And my mind darkened with a confusion of realities and unrealities: the knowledge of my own sins, and the false humility which makes men say that they cannot do the things that they must do, cannot reach the level that they must reach: the cowardice that says: "I am satisfied to save my soul, to keep out of mortal sin," but which means, by those words: "I do not want to give up my sins and my attachments." But Lax said: "No. All that is necessary to be a saint is to want to be one. Don't you believe that

God will make you what He created you to be, if you will consent to let Him do it?" (pg. 260)

Thomas Merton became convinced that Robert Lax was right. We were created to become saints, but it is something we must want to become. He also came to realize we cannot make ourselves saints. We can only open ourselves to the holiness of God – for God alone is holy. As he says 11 years later in his book *The Sign of Jonas* (pg 162): "A saint is not so much a man who realizes that he possesses virtues and sanctity as one who is overwhelmed by the sanctity of God." We become holy by "sharing in his being" and "rising above the level of everything that is not God."

Sharing in God's being is the same as the concept frequently used in Scripture, especially in St. John's gospel. It is the idea of sharing in his life, which comes to us through the sacraments. Saint John tells us today: "See what love the Father has bestowed on us that we may be called the children of God. Yet that is what we are." The term "saint" is often used in the New Testament to refer to Christians in general, for they who share God's life are holy (that's what "saint" means). Very early on it was used to designate people whose holiness was outstanding, especially the martyrs. Today the official list of saints' names is close to 7000 people whose holiness the Church officially recognizes. They give us heroic examples of having faithfully followed Christ. We all have heroes, especially as we grow up. It's good to have people as heroes, people who excel in living holy lives and not just sports figures or rock stars. It's good also to have friends in high places when we need help. We often ask our friends to pray for us in difficult times, why not ask those whom we know are special friends of God. We don't adore saints (as we are sometimes accused of doing), we adore only God, but we also honor the saints' holy lives and ask for their prayers. Today we honor all those who haven't made it to the major leagues of sainthood, parents, grandparents, friends who have inspired us and helped us along our journey to God. They are part of "that great multitude which no one could count, from every nation, race, people and tongue" which our first reading from Revelation told us about today. We ask their prayers, we ask them to help us to someday be with them as saints to enjoy the holiness and glory for which God created us.

Amen.

All Souls
November 2, 2008

INTRODUCTION – (2 Maccabees 12:43-46; Romans 5:5-11; John 6:37-40) Our first reading, from the book of Maccabees, comes from about 100 years before Christ. At that time in history the Greeks were the dominant power and they were trying to get the Jews to abandon their faith and follow the beliefs of the pagans. Those who would not give in were persecuted and put to death. The loyal Jews fought back. In one of their battles, many Jews were killed. As they were being buried, it was found that they had small statues of pagan gods attached to their garments. These Jews were loyal to their Jewish beliefs, but they had, to some extent, given in to paganism. Just in case those pagan gods were real, they were carrying with them statues of pagan gods to give them protection. Their leader, Judas Maccabeus, took up a collection to send to Jerusalem for sacrifices to be offered up to the Lord for those people. He believed their hearts were, in general, in the right place, but for the weakness in their faith they had to be forgiven. In this piece of history from 100 B.C., we can see the beginnings of the belief that our prayers can help those who have died, a belief that is still part of our faith.

HOMILY – Praying for our deceased relatives and friends is what our feast of All Souls is about today. However, I had the hardest time getting started with today's homily. I kept putting it off. It's not as if I do not believe in praying for friends and relatives who have died. I do it all the time and it has been a tradition in the Church from the beginning, and even before that as we heard in our first reading.

I think the difficulty I had in developing my homily comes from two sources. First, many people don't like to hear about death and what might come afterwards. We know we can't avoid it, but my sense is that many people believe that if they don't think about it, it won't happen, at least not for a long time. My suspicion is that my father was that way. I constantly tried to get him to make a will but he never did. As a CPA he would have known it was a good idea. I think making a will would have made the prospect of his own death too concrete and too real for him to deal with.

The second reason today's homily was hard was that I would have to talk about Purgatory. It's an idea that many Christians deny. I remember once I was helping a family prepare the liturgy for their deceased father and they insisted "absolutely no mention of Purgatory." It's as if it were a bad word. They wanted to think their father was perfect, I guess, and was already in heaven. Most of us would like to believe that our loved ones go straight to heaven when they die – period. If this were true, then they would not need our prayers. If they went to the other place, God forbid, our prayers would do them no good. The Church teaches, in every Mass we have for a person who died and in today's feast, that our prayers do help our relatives and friends who have left this world as they journey to eternal life.

Purgatory, among all the mysteries and beliefs of the Church is an extremely logical and comforting doctrine. It's logical if we ask ourselves how many of us think we will be perfect when we die. There may even be some who are perfect right now. I would ask them to identify themselves, but if they're perfect, they will also be too humble to do so. Even those who lived a good life may still have a little room for improvement, they may still not love God or others quite enough. That's where Purgatory comes in – it's an opportunity to grow into the most loving, most holy person we can possibly be. As a result we would then be filled with God's peace and joy and love to the fullest extent. Luther rejected the idea of Purgatory because of the abuse of indulgences at the time. Today, the concept of Purgatory has been rejected by many because of all the negative images of suffering and punishment that we grew up with. Actually, I think for the souls in Purgatory, happiness far outweighs the unhappiness. Their salvation is sure, they are more closely united with God than they had ever experienced before in their lives, they are on their way to the enjoyment of God's kingdom in the fullest possible way. But they're not there yet and that's the painful part. If you read the book, "The Five People You Meet in Heaven," I think you get a good, practical image of Purgatory. It's not a religious book, it's very entertaining and it pictured for me what Purgatory might be like as we work out issues, regrets, hurts, conflicts, etc., that we might take with us when we die.

To demonstrate that Purgatory makes so much sense,

I think that those who deny Purgatory have had to find a substitute for it in their thinking about the next life. For many that substitute is reincarnation. In reincarnation a person supposedly keeps working for greater and greater purity and holiness until they are ready to be perfectly one with God. However, reincarnation comes from Hinduism. Actually a Hindu does not look forward to reincarnation because they don't want to have to pass through this world of pain and suffering one more time. I suspect the notion of reincarnation has been adopted by many Westerners, even Christians, because it fits our culture of "buy now, pay later." They figure they can live any way they want and can postpone having to pay any consequences. Our faith tells us, "now is the acceptable time, now is the day of salvation." God gives us what we need in this life to help us know him and serve him in this life. If we do not do it perfectly, Purgatory is there to finish the job. Today, we renew our faith in life after death. Today too we renew our belief in the power of prayer to help our loved ones, even those who are no longer among us, for in Christ they are still one with us. With Christ our great high priest, we offer now the greatest prayer there is, the Eucharist.

32nd Sunday in Ordinary Time
November 11, 2012

INTRODUCTION – (1 Kings 17:10-16; Hebrews 9:24-28; Mark 12:38-44) I want to begin by saying something about the second reading. The author of the Letter to the Hebrews was interested in showing the superiority of Jesus' sacrifice over Old Testament sacrifices. The author of the Letter especially focuses on the most important Jewish sacrifice in the entire year, the sacrifice offered on the Day of Atonement (Yom Kippur). The Jewish Temple existed for around 1000 years, and while sacrifices were offered every day, there was one special day on which the High Priest, and only the High Priest, entered the Holy of Holies, the innermost sanctuary of the Temple. At no other time during the year could anyone enter the Holy of Holies. The High Priest would sprinkle the blood of animals in that Holy Place and ask forgiveness for his sins and those of the people of Israel. Part of the ceremony involved the High Priest holding his hands over a goat and placing the sins of the people on this goat. The goat was then taken into the desert to die, symbolizing that the people's sins were gone. This is where the word "scape goat" comes from. It was a day when all of Israel would pray and would fast from food and drink. Even though there is no Temple, Jews still fast on that day and spend extra time in prayer asking God to forgive their sins. The Letter to the Hebrews emphasizes that Christ's sacrifice for sins took place only once and it didn't need to be offered again and again since it was a perfect sacrifice. We participate in this perfect sacrifice of Christ each time we come to Mass.

Our first reading will make more sense if we know that the events that are described in the reading happened during a severe famine. We have to marvel at the faith of the widow in our first reading, a faith that is reflected in the offering of another poor widow in today's gospel.

HOMILY – The showiness of some of the Jewish leaders is contrasted with the humility of a poor widow. Jesus does not tell us all Jewish leaders were that way, wearing fancy dress, looking for recognition and preferential treatment, but surely some were. Jesus does not tell us that those who made generous offerings to the

Temple were show-offs (although they could hardly hide the loud noise their many coins would make as they fell into the metallic offering boxes that stood in the court of the Temple. Our parishioner and expert on currency, Gene Hessler, informs us in his book on the subject that paper money would not be around for several more centuries. Jesus did not condemn those who gave generously. Their generous gifts kept the Temple in good repair and supported the priests and Levites who ministered daily. There is nothing wrong with having a beautiful space dedicated to the worship of God. Jesus had great respect for the Temple. We like to have a beautiful church to remind us of God's grandeur and to inspire us to know we are in a special place. The person, however, who most impressed Jesus was not a person who gave lots of gold but a poor widow who gave two little coins worth about two or three cents. It reminds us that when we come to church what Jesus notices most about us is the love that's in our hearts. It also reminds us that we can't judge one another.

We are all affected by people's behavior – in that it is prayerful, pleasing, respectful or that it is distracting and annoying. That is not being judgmental, it's just stating how I am affected by something. But we can't judge another's heart. Only Jesus can. Just as the woman in our first reading was blessed by her kindness to the prophet, we can be sure that whatever love we bring with us to offer to God will be blessed abundantly by the God of love. Jesus said anyone who gives even a cup of cold water in his name will not lose his or her reward.

I think today would be a great opportunity to thank our people for their generosity to St. Boniface. I have been overwhelmed by the generosity of so many of our people – since last year when we had an appeal for increased offertory support and this year for our capital campaign to brighten up the church and take about 50 years of dirt off the walls and ceiling. So I thank you and assure you the Lord, who will not allow us to surpass him in generosity and who generously gave himself for us, will bless you generously for your goodness. Amen.

33rd Sunday in Ordinary Time
November 18, 2012

INTRODUCTION – (Daniel 12:1-3; Heb 10:11-14; Mk 13:24-32) Most of us, I am sure, are familiar with the last book of the Bible: the Book of Revelation. Since the entire New Testament was originally written in Greek, and the Book of Revelation began with the Greek word "apocalypses," which means revelation, the book is also referred to as the Apocalypse. What most people do not know is there are a number of other passages in the Bible that are apocalyptic in nature; that is, they reveal to God's people what is going to take place. Usually they were written during a time when God's people were being persecuted. They tried to give hope to God's people that if they remained faithful to God their sufferings would soon be at an end and God, or perhaps God's delegate, the Messiah, would overcome God's enemies and would initiate an era of peace. This era was known as God's reign or God's kingdom. Our first reading today, from the Book of Daniel, written about 165 BC, is an example of apocalyptic writing. It was a time of Jewish persecution. Preceding today's reading, the Book of Daniel describes several visions Daniel had about the immediate future of God's people. The vision predicted that the Syrians would try to destroy the faith of the Jewish people and would persecute and kill those Jews who were faithful. The time was described as "unsurpassed in distress." Today's passage predicts that during that time the Archangel Michael, the guardian of the Jews, would come to the aid of God's people. The passage contains a clear belief in resurrection to glory for those who remained faithful and a resurrection to ignominy for those who had not.

HOMILY – In my introduction I spoke of apocalyptic writing in the Book of Revelation and in the Book of Daniel. Today's gospel is also apocalyptic in nature. Jesus would have spoken these words during a time when the Jews were subject to Roman rule and they sought their independence. Mark would have recalled these words of Jesus some 35 or 40 years later as he was writing his gospel for his community of Christians who were suffering persecution from both the Romans and the Jews. These words were meant to assure Jesus' listeners as well as Mark's community that Jesus would return again and usher in the kingdom of God, an era of everlasting peace for those who have remained faithful. The first half of today's gospel uses images from the Old Testament: images of the universe decomposing, the sun and moon growing dark and the stars falling from the sky, the Son of Man appearing in power and glory and gathering together his chosen ones. The second half of our gospel attempts to assure God's people that their sufferings would not last much longer. Their expectation was that Jesus would return very soon and their suffering would be over. I think perhaps that is what Jesus is speaking symbolically when he says, "this generation will not pass away before all these things come to pass." Even though Jesus is encouraging perseverance in our faith and wants us to know the suffering will end soon, he also adds no one knows when it will come. It is necessary to be ready for it – a message that is repeated a number of times in the gospels.

I want to say a word about another group of Jews who

lived roughly 200 years before Christ and who were probably annihilated by the Romans around the year 70 AD (the same year the Temple in Jerusalem was destroyed). I'm talking about the Essenes. They were an apocalyptic community living in the desert near the Dead Sea. They were preparing by prayer and study and asceticism for the coming of God's kingdom. They looked forward to the coming of two Messiahs, one a priest, a descendant of Aaron and one a king, a descendant of David. The group regarded themselves as the last generation of people on earth. Their War Scroll indicates they would participate in the conflict at the end of days that would occur between the sons of light and the sons of darkness. The redeemed, primarily the Essenes, who referred to themselves as the Yahad, would dwell in everlasting joy in eternity.

I mention this because an exhibit just opened at the Museum Center displaying some of the Essenes' writings, documents that are about 2000 years old and older. These documents, called the Dead Sea Scrolls, make up a collection of about 600 manuscripts, consisting of about 10 complete scrolls and thousands of fragments. I am holding a 600 page book of translations of the various scrolls. You can see from this how much material became available to the world in 1947 when the scrolls were first discovered (quite by accident). This is amazing when we realize that before 1947, when the Dead Sea Scrolls were found, the oldest known copy of any Old Testament Hebrew manuscript was written in 895 AD (the Cairo Prophets). Now we have manuscripts that are 1000 years older than the oldest one we knew. These documents are not only important because of their antiquity but also because they shed light on a whole segment of the Jewish population at the time of Jesus whom we had previously known about only through a few comments by historians.

John the Baptist may actually have been a part of this group at one time. With the Scrolls we know a great deal more about the time and culture when Jesus lived.

There is no way all these documents will be on display at the Museum Center. I haven't seen the exhibit yet, but I did see it when I was in Jerusalem. Even though you won't be able to read the Hebrew or Aramaic in which most of the Scrolls were written, it's still awesome to see and it's interesting to hear the story of how they were found. They do have a connection with Cincinnati. When it looked like Israel would be in a war in 1969, Nelson Glueck, president of the Hebrew Union College (HUC), was commissioned to take photographs of the scrolls and keep the negatives. For 20 years these negatives (1500 of them) were kept secret here in Cincinnati. When the team of scholars who were supposed to be translating the Scrolls took so long to come out with a translation, a scholar named Hershel Shanks gave a lecture here in Cincinnati and revealed the secret about the existence of the negatives for the Scrolls. A professor at HUC and a student began translating the Scrolls and published their work. This got things going with the academic community. There is so much more that could be said, but if you get to visit the exhibit, you'll learn a lot more. Amen.

Feast of Christ the King
November 25, 2012

INTRODUCTION – (Daniel 7:13-14; Rev 1:5-8; John 18:33-37) Last week I spoke about apocalyptic writing and its intent to give hope and encouragement to God's people during difficult times. The Book of Revelation, aka the Apocalypse in the New Testament, and the

Book of Daniel in the Old Testament are examples of apocalyptic writing. Again this week we hear from the book of Daniel. This book was written during a time when the Jews were being severely persecuted for their faith. As in all apocalyptic writing, today's reading describes how God would triumph in the end. God would establish a kingdom, which would replace all other kingdoms and God's kingdom would be everlasting. God is here described as "the Ancient One." His kingdom would be ruled by one who is described as "a son of man." God would give this "son of man" dominion, glory and kingship. The term "son of man" means literally a human being, but today's passage gives new meaning and mystery to this expression. You might recall "son of man" was the favorite title Jesus used to describe himself.

HOMILY – The other morning I woke up asking myself this bizarre question: "What would I do if I alone had knowledge of where some weapons of mass destruction were hidden and I were captured by terrorists who were torturing me to get me to tell them where the weapons were hidden? Would I give in and tell them?" The idea was frightening – probably prompted by a crazy dream, but I answered my own question: I could never give away such information that would cause harm for so many people.

Then an opposite idea struck me: "What if I had some knowledge that I knew would help millions of people, but my life would be endangered were I to reveal that knowledge? Would I reveal it anyway?" Of course.

Maybe I was having delusions of grandeur, but this thought gave me some insight into Jesus' death. He had a vision and a knowledge that he was certain would save billions of people. This is why he came, to share with us what he knew about the kingdom of God. What he announced would allow people to participate in this kingdom forever. He began his public ministry proclaiming God's kingdom – that it was near at hand. He demonstrated that he spoke with power and authority through expelling demons, healing sick people, feeding hungry crowds, calming storms, walking on water and even raising some people back to life. Everything about him proved that he was not some kind of a nut case. Some people decided that he was crazy when he talked about the Eucharist and they walked away from him. But he was attracting enough people that those in power felt their position threatened and they knew the only way they could silence him was to have him put to death. They took him before the one person who had power to execute him, Pontius Pilate. However, Jesus could not stop proclaiming his message for he knew his message was too important to the world. People needed to hear it no matter what the consequences. To proclaim the kingdom of God was what he came for and he was its king. "For this I was born, for this I came into the world, to testify to the truth," he told the Roman procurator.

Often when we read about or hear about things going on in the news, we ask "where are you God?" "Why are these things happening?" We forget his kingdom does not belong to this world, but it does exist. Our challenge is to believe in the kingdom, to believe in its king and to follow the way he has shown us.

I thank all of you for being here today, for your faith, for responding to Jesus' invitation to enter into his kingdom and for the support your faith gives to me and to others who are traveling the road to eternal life along with you. I am grateful to be in your company as we make that journey together. Amen.

September 25, 2014

My dear beloved priests,

I give my heart to Jesus and Mary with you in love.

In today's world we need to listen to Our Lady of Fatima the Queen of Peace.

We can be united in one heart in the Hearts of Jesus and Mary.

Please pray the prayers on the enclosed brochure praying for the priests, the Church and the world.

I feel it is a great message Our Lady of Fatima gave –

Excerpts from *The Spirituality of Fatima*
by Fr. Edward Carter, S.J.

Before Jacinta died, she told of other messages given her (during her illness) by Mary:

> *Tell everybody that God gives graces through the Immaculate Heart of Mary. Tell them to ask grace from her, and that the Heart of Jesus wishes to be venerated together with the Immaculate Heart of Mary. Ask them to plead for peace from the Immaculate Heart of Mary, for the Lord has confided the peace of the world to her.*[19]

19. Our Lady's Peace Plan, op cit., p.6.

If we want the world to change we must give our hearts to Jesus and be united.

Father Carter, S.J. when he started the Shepherds of Christ said Jesus wanted him to spread the Priestly Newsletter every other month to priests. He did this 20 years ago and with his Newsletters and Newsletter Books and other priests, we have circulated 17,000,000 Priestly Newsletters in books and loose in these 20 years. He would send them to 85,000 priests every other month.

Father Carter, S.J. then gave us the Shepherds of Christ Prayers centered in devotion to the Sacred Heart and Immaculate Heart praying for the priests, the Church and the world. Fr. Carter had a doctorate in theology and his Priestly Newsletters were for priests and are in 3 Volumes of Priestly Newsletters. They are so good. Short readings quoting scripture and Popes and Saints and very gifted theologian priests who wrote tremendous works. You can order these Priestly Newsletters Books and use them as short meditations every day - on the spiritual life. They are on topics like Death/Resurrection, Love, Christ in us, Priesthood using Pope John Paul II and the Church Documents, Encyclicals in very well simple reading.

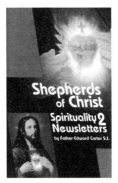

Fr. Joe, my brother, celebrated being a priest for 50 years in May this year. This is his eighth book of Sunday homilies, Rooted in the Bread of Life, the Word and the Eucharist – Fr. Joe gives us a gift in his homilies to know more about the time-line of the Old Testament, how the Old Testament prefigures the New Testament and how Jesus truly is our friend and our strength. Father Joe has a Bachelor's and Masters' Degrees in Philosophy and a Master's in Divinity degree, also a Masters in Psychology. He was head of the Cathedral Deanery for many years and holds a license as Professional Clinical Counselor from the State of Ohio Counselor and Social Worker Board.

He inspires his parishioners with homilies found in his books. They are not only practical, but also filled with light humor and a sense of hope, the hope of living out the Gospel despite today's challenges.

These Homily Books can be a Guiding Light for you as they have been for many others.

Fr. Carter, S.J., our founder, began the prayer chapters praying for the priests, the Church and the world 20 years ago. We have these, Shepherds of Christ prayers, in 8 languages with the Church's *Imprimatur* – English, French, Spanish, Portuguese, Italian, Polish, Burmese and an Indian dialect.

Fr. Carter said Mary said at Fatima, that until a sufficient number of people have given their hearts to Jesus and Mary we won't have peace in the world.

We have 24 hour adoration before the exposed Eucharist in our Church, St. Anthony, in China, Indiana. We pray for you there 24 hours a day and every night at 6:20 pm in community for our beloved priests, the Church and the world and have since 1998.

I pray with the community, 8 days - every month in retreats for you our beloved priests and we usually have about 6 Masses that priests come and say for us every month while on retreat praying for the priests, the Church and the world.

I am Rita Robinson Ring, co-founder of the Shepherds of Christ Movement – this Movement is over 20 years old. The Church is such a gift – I wrote this song about our beloved priests.

Song: *A Priest is a Gift from God*

A Priest Is a Gift from God

by Rita Ring

REFRAIN

C   F   C   Am   C

A priest is a gift from God. A priest is a gift from God.

F   C   F   G

This is My Bod - y, This is My Blood, A

VERSES 1, 3

C   F   C   C   F   G

priest is a gift from God.
1. Come to Me, My chil - dren,
3. Come to Me, chil-dren of God,

C   F   G   C   F   G

I want to pos-sess your soul, I love you so ten - der - ly,
I want to pos-sess your soul, I give My-self to___ you

C   F   G   C   F   C

I want you to love Me too, A priest is a gift from God.
in the Ho - ly Eu -cha-rist, A priest is a gift from God.

F   G   C   F   C

I tell you My chil - dren, a priest is a gift from God. To -
I tell you My chil - dren, a priest is a gift from God. To -

F   G   C   F   G

day is the day the Lord has made, Wake, My chil-dren from your sleep,
day is the day the Lord has made, Wake, My chil-dren from your sleep,

Song: *A Song from Jesus*

A Song from Jesus

by Rita Ring

REFRAIN

I come to you with great-est love, I
am your lov-ing Sav-ior. I am your God, I
died for you, I come to you this day.

VERSES

1. You are My pre - cious lit - tle one, I
2. Reach out to Me and do not fear, I

love you oh so dear - ly. Come close to Me, My
want to be so close to you. You are My child, My

lit - tle one, I loved you to My death.
pre - cious one, I love you ten - der - ly.

Song: *I Love You Jesus*

I Love You Jesus

by Rita Ring

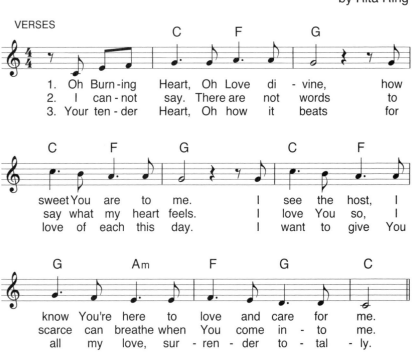

VERSES

1. Oh Burn-ing Heart, Oh Love di-vine, how
2. I can-not say. There are not words to
3. Your ten-der Heart, Oh how it beats for

sweet You are to me. I see the host, I
say what my heart feels. I love You so, I
love of each this day. I want to give You

know You're here to love and care for me.
scarce can breathe when You come in-to me.
all my love, sur-ren-der to-tal-ly.

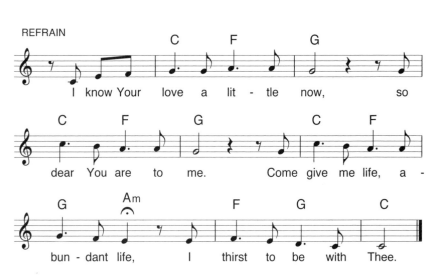

REFRAIN

I know Your love a lit-tle now, so

dear You are to me. Come give me life, a-

bun-dant life, I thirst to be with Thee.

Please pray these prayers with us and help us spread them –

When people give their hearts to Jesus and Mary, they are in one heart in the Father's will – ONE MIND IN JESUS

We have these consecration cards we spread to school children.

Consecration to Mary

Dear Mary, my holy mother, I love you so much and I give you my heart. Help me to love God. Help me to love my neighbor as a child of God. Help me to love myself as a child of God.

Amen

2009 © SHEPHERDS OF CHRIST PUBLICATIONS

Consecration to Jesus

Dear Sacred Heart of Jesus, I love You so much and I give You my heart. Help me to love God. Help me to love my neighbor as a child of God. Help me to love myself as a child of God.

Amen

2009 © SHEPHERDS OF CHRIST PUBLICATIONS

And we supply schools with cute rosaries for school children.

Song: *The Rosary Song*

The Rosary Song

by Rita Rin

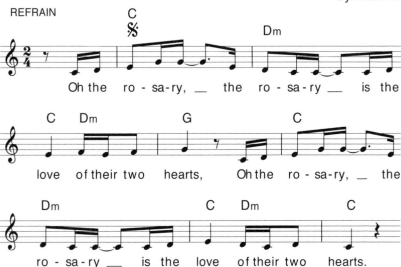

REFRAIN

Oh the ro - sa-ry, __ the ro - sa-ry __ is the love of their two hearts, Oh the ro - sa-ry, __ the ro - sa-ry __ is the love of their two hearts.

VERSES 1-4

1. A - ve Ma - ri - a, A - ve Ma - ri - a. Oh the
2. Je - sus we love You, Ma - ry we love__ you. Oh the
3. This is her peace plan, Chil-dren must pray__ it. Oh the
4. We turn to Ma - ry, She is the Queen of Peace. Oh the

VERSE 5

No left hand

5. Oh Sa-cred Heart di - vine, Oh heart of Ma-ry pure,

A - ve Ma - ri - a, We love to pray it! Oh the

Please help us start the prayer chapters.

We spread these Morning Offering – Say Daily Cards to the Nursing homes.

SAY DAILY

GOD, I GIVE YOU MY LIFE IN UNION WITH THE MASS AS AN OFFERING FOR THE SOULS, THE CHURCH AND THE PRIESTS.

HELP US!

We invite you to be in one mind and one heart with us in the Hearts of Jesus and Mary praying united to the Mass for the priests, the Church and the world.

Rita Robinson Ring, Co-founder
Shepherds of Christ Ministries

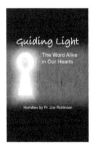

Help us get these books to our priests. Please give a donation if you can and pray for this work and pray the prayers on the brochure for the priests, the Church and the world.

Help us spread these books to priests, deacons, sisters, brothers, music ministers, principals, directors of religious education –

This is a gift that gives every Sunday and keeps giving in helping build the body of Christ, the Church.

IN REMEMBRANCE
OF MY
FIFTIETH ANNIVERSARY
OF PRIESTLY ORDINATION

Rev. JOSEPH A. ROBINSON
1964   MAY   2014

Let us Pray for one another

"This is My Body, This is My Blood."

Prayer Before the
Holy Sacrifice of the Mass

Let me be a holy sacrifice and unite with God in the sacrament of His greatest love.

I want to be one in Him in this act of love, where He gives Himself to me and I give myself as a sacrifice to Him. Let me be a holy sacrifice as I become one with Him in this my act of greatest love to Him.

Let me unite with Him more, that I may more deeply love Him. May I help make reparation to His adorable Heart and the heart of His Mother, Mary. With greatest love, I offer myself to You and pray that You will accept my sacrifice of greatest love. I give myself to You and unite in Your gift of Yourself to me. Come and possess my soul.

Cleanse me, strengthen me, heal me. Dear Holy Spirit act in the heart of Mary to make me more and more like Jesus.

Father, I offer this my sacrifice, myself united to Jesus in the Holy Spirit to You. Help me to love God more deeply in this act of my greatest love.

Give me the grace to grow in my knowledge, love and service of You and for this to be my greatest participation in the Mass. Give me the greatest graces to love You so deeply in this Mass, You who are so worthy of my love.

– *Mass Book*, December 27, 1995

Shepherds of Christ Associates

PRAYER MANUAL

Shepherds of Christ Publications
China, Indiana

Imprimi Potest: Rev. Bradley M. Schaeffer, S.J.
Provincial
Chicago Province, The Society of Jesus

Imprimatur: Most Rev. Carl K. Moeddel
Auxiliary Bishop
Archdiocese of Cincinnati

The Shepherds of Christ Associates Prayer Manual is published by
Shepherds of Christ Publications, an arm of Shepherds of Christ Ministries,
P.O. Box 627 China, Indiana 47250 USA.

Founder, Shepherds of Christ Ministries:
Father Edward J. Carter, S.J.

For more information contact:
Shepherds of Christ Associates
P.O. Box 627
China, Indiana 47250- USA
Tel. 812-273-8405
Toll Free: 1-888-211-3041
Fax 812-273-3182

First Printing, September 1994
Second Printing, November 1994
Third Printing, November 1995
Fourth Printing, March 1996

Chapter Meeting
Prayer Format

The prayer format below should be followed at chapter meetings of *Shepherds of Christ Associates*. All prayers, not just those said specifically for priests, should include the intention of praying for all the needs of priests the world over.

1. **Hymns.** Hymns may be sung at any point of the prayer part of the meeting.

2. **Holy Spirit Prayer.** Come, Holy Spirit, almighty Sanctifier, God of love, who filled the Virgin Mary with grace, who wonderfully changed the hearts of the apostles, who endowed all Your martyrs with miraculous courage, come and sanctify us. Enlighten our minds, strengthen our wills, purify our consciences, rectify our judgment, set our hearts on fire, and preserve us from the misfortunes of resisting Your inspirations. Amen.

3. **The Rosary.**

4. **Salve Regina.** "Hail Holy Queen, Mother of mercy, our life, our sweetness, and our hope. To you do we cry, poor banished children of Eve. To you do we send up our sighs, our mourning, our weeping in this vale of tears. Turn, then, most gracious advocate, your eyes of mercy toward us and after this, our exile, show unto us the blessed fruit of your womb, Jesus, O clement, O loving, O sweet Virgin Mary. Amen."

5. **The Memorare.** "Remember, O most gracious Virgin Mary, that never was it known that anyone who fled to your protection, implored your help, or sought your intercession was left unaided. Inspired by this confidence, I fly unto you, O Virgin of virgins, my

Mother. To you I come, before you I stand, sinful and sorrowful. O Mother of the Word Incarnate, despise not my petitions, but, in your mercy, hear and answer me. Amen."

6. **Seven Hail Marys in honor of the Seven Sorrows of Mary.** Mary has promised very special graces to those who do this on a daily basis. Included in the promises of Our Lady for those who practice this devotion is her pledge to give special assistance at the hour of death, including the sight of her face. The seven sorrows are:

(1) The first sorrow: the prophecy of Simeon (Hail Mary).

(2) The second sorrow: the flight into Egypt (Hail Mary).

(3) The third sorrow: the loss of the Child Jesus in the temple (Hail Mary).

(4) The fourth sorrow: Jesus and Mary meet on the way to the cross (Hail Mary).

(5) The fifth sorrow: Jesus dies on the cross (Hail Mary).

(6) The sixth sorrow: Jesus is taken down from the cross and laid in Mary's arms (Hail Mary).

(7) The seventh sorrow: the burial of Jesus (Hail Mary).

7. **Litany of the Blessed Virgin Mary.**
Lord, have mercy on us.
Christ, have mercy on us.
Lord, have mercy on us. Christ, hear us.
Christ, graciously hear us.
God, the Father of heaven, *have mercy on us.*
God, the Son, Redeemer of the world, *have mercy on us.*
God, the Holy Spirit, *have mercy on us.*

Holy Trinity, one God, *have mercy on us.*
Holy Mary, *pray for us* (repeat after each invocation).
Holy Mother of God,
Holy Virgin of virgins,
Mother of Christ,
Mother of the Church,
Mother of divine grace,
Mother most pure,
Mother most chaste,
Mother inviolate,
Mother undefiled,
Mother most amiable,
Mother most admirable,
Mother of good counsel,
Mother of our Creator,
Mother of our Savior,
Virgin most prudent,
Virgin most venerable,
Virgin most renowned,
Virgin most powerful,
Virgin most merciful,
Virgin most faithful,
Mirror of justice,
Seat of wisdom,
Cause of our joy,
Spiritual vessel,
Vessel of honor,
Singular vessel of devotion,
Mystical rose,
Tower of David,
Tower of ivory,
House of gold,
Ark of the Covenant,
Gate of heaven,

Morning star,
Health of the sick,
Refuge of sinners,
Comforter of the afflicted,
Help of Christians,
Queen of angels,
Queen of patriarchs,
Queen of prophets,
Queen of apostles,
Queen of martyrs,
Queen of confessors,
Queen of virgins,
Queen of all saints,
Queen conceived without original sin,
Queen assumed into heaven,
Queen of the most holy rosary,
Queen of families,
Queen of peace,
Lamb of God, who take away the sins of the world,
  spare us, O Lord.
Lamb of God, who take away the sins of the world,
  graciously hear us, O Lord.
Lamb of God, who take away the sins of the world,
  have mercy on us.
Pray for us, O holy Mother of God,
  that we may be made worthy of the promises of Christ.

Let us pray: Grant, we beseech You, O Lord God, that we Your servants may enjoy perpetual health of mind and body and, by the glorious intercession of the blessed Mary, ever virgin, be delivered from present sorrow, and obtain eternal joy. Through Christ our Lord. Amen.

We fly to your patronage, O holy Mother of God. Despise not our petitions in our necessities, but deliver us always from all dangers, O glorious and blessed Virgin. Amen.

8. **Prayer to St. Joseph.** St. Joseph, guardian of Jesus and chaste spouse of Mary, you passed your life in perfect fulfillment of duty. You supported the Holy Family of Nazareth with the work of your hands. Kindly protect those who trustingly turn to you. You know their aspirations, their hardships, their hopes; and they turn to you because they know you will understand and protect them. You too have known trial, labor, and weariness. But, even amid the worries of material life, your soul was filled with deep peace and sang out in true joy through intimacy with the Son of God entrusted to you, and with Mary, His tender Mother. Amen.

— *(Pope John XXIII)*

9. **Litany of the Sacred Heart, promises of the Sacred Heart.**
Lord, have mercy on us.
   Christ, have mercy on us.
Lord, have mercy on us. Christ, hear us.
   Christ, graciously hear us.
God the Father of heaven,
   have mercy on us (repeat after each invocation).
God the Son, Redeemer of the world,
God the Holy Spirit,
Holy Trinity, one God,
Heart of Jesus, Son of the eternal Father,
Heart of Jesus, formed by the Holy Spirit in the womb of the Virgin Mother,
Heart of Jesus, substantially united to the Word of God,
Heart of Jesus, of infinite majesty,

Heart of Jesus, sacred temple of God,

Heart of Jesus, tabernacle of the Most High,

Heart of Jesus, house of God and gate of heaven,

Heart of Jesus, burning furnace of charity,

Heart of Jesus, abode of justice and love,

Heart of Jesus, full of goodness and love,

Heart of Jesus, abyss of all virtues,

Heart of Jesus, most worthy of all praise,

Heart of Jesus, king and center of all hearts,

Heart of Jesus, in whom are all the treasures of wisdom and knowledge,

Heart of Jesus, in whom dwells the fullness of divinity,

Heart of Jesus, in whom the Father is well pleased,

Heart of Jesus, of whose fullness we have all received,

Heart of Jesus, desire of the everlasting hills,

Heart of Jesus, patient and most merciful,

Heart of Jesus, enriching all who invoke You,

Heart of Jesus, fountain of life and holiness,

Heart of Jesus, propitiation for our sins,

Heart of Jesus, loaded down with opprobrium,

Heart of Jesus, bruised for our offenses,

Heart of Jesus, obedient even to death,

Heart of Jesus, pierced with a lance,

Heart of Jesus, source of all consolation,

Heart of Jesus, our life and reconciliation,

Heart of Jesus, victim of sin,

Heart of Jesus, salvation of those who hope in You,

Heart of Jesus, hope of those who die in You,

Heart of Jesus, delight of all the saints,

Lamb of God, Who take away the sins of the world,
spare us, O Lord.

Lamb of God, Who take away the sins of the world,

graciously hear us, O Lord.
Lamb of God, Who take away the sins of the world,
  have mercy on us.
Jesus, meek and humble of heart,
  make our hearts like unto Yours.

Let us pray: O almighty and eternal God, look upon the Heart of Your dearly beloved Son and upon the praise and satisfaction He offers You in behalf of sinners and, being appeased, grant pardon to those who seek Your mercy, in the name of the same Jesus Christ, Your Son, Who lives and reigns with You, in the unity of the Holy Spirit, world without end. Amen.

Promises of Our Lord to those devoted to His Sacred Heart (these should be read by the prayer leader):

(1) I will give them all the graces necessary in their state of life.
(2) I will establish peace in their homes.
(3) I will comfort them in all their afflictions.
(4) I will be their refuge during life and above all in death.
(5) I will bestow a large blessing on all their undertakings.
(6) Sinners shall find in My Heart the source and the infinite ocean of mercy.
(7) Tepid souls shall grow fervent.
(8) Fervent souls shall quickly mount to high perfection.
(9) I will bless every place where a picture of My Heart shall be set up and honored.
(10) I will give to priests the gift of touching the most hardened hearts.
(11) Those who promote this devotion shall have their names written in My Heart, never to be blotted out.

(12) I promise you in the excessive mercy of My Heart that My all-powerful love will grant to all those who communicate on the first Friday in nine consecutive months the grace of final penitence; they shall not die in My disgrace nor without receiving their sacraments; My divine Heart shall be their safe refuge in this last moment.

10. **Prayer for Priests.** "Lord Jesus, Chief Shepherd of the Flock, we pray that in the great love and mercy of Your Sacred Heart You attend to all the needs of Your priest-shepherds throughout the world. We ask that You draw back to Your Heart all those priests who have seriously strayed from Your path, that You rekindle the desire for holiness in the hearts of those priests who have become lukewarm, and that You continue to give Your fervent priests the desire for the highest holiness. United with Your Heart and Mary's Heart, we ask that You take this petition to Your heavenly Father in the unity of the Holy Spirit. Amen."

11. **Prayer for all members of the Shepherds of Christ Associates.** "Dear Jesus, we ask Your special blessings on all members of Shepherds of Christ Associates. Continue to enlighten them regarding the very special privilege and responsibility you have given them as members of Your movement, Shepherds of Christ Associates. Draw them ever closer to Your Heart and to Your Mother's Heart. Allow them to more and more realize the great and special love of Your Hearts for each of them as unique individuals. Give them the grace to respond to Your love and Mary's love with an increased love of their own. As they dwell in Your Heart and Mary's Heart, abundantly care for all their needs and those of their loved ones. We make our

prayer through You to the Father, in the Holy Spirit, with Mary our Mother at our side. Amen."

12. **Prayer for the spiritual and financial success of the priestly newsletter.** "Father, we ask Your special blessings upon the priestly newsletter, Shepherds of Christ. We ask that You open the priest-readers to the graces You wish to give them through this chosen instrument of Your Son. We also ask that You provide for the financial needs of the newsletter and the Shepherds of Christ Associates. We make our prayer through Jesus, in the Holy Spirit, with Mary at our side. Amen."

13. **Prayer for all members of the human family.** "Heavenly Father, we ask Your blessings on all Your children the world over. Attend to all their needs. We ask Your special assistance for all those marginalized people, all those who are so neglected and forgotten. United with our Mother Mary, we make this petition to You through Jesus and in the Holy Spirit. Amen."

14. **Prayer to St. Michael and our Guardian Angels:** "St. Michael the Archangel, defend us in battle. Be our safeguard against the wickedness and snares of the devil. May God rebuke him, we humbly pray, and do thou, O prince of the heavenly hosts, by the power of God, cast into hell Satan and all the other evil spirits who prowl about the world seeking the ruin of souls. Amen."
"Angel of God, my guardian dear, to whom God's love commits me here, ever this day be at my side, to light and guard, to rule and guide. Amen."

15. **Pause for silent, personal prayer.** This should last at least five minutes.

16. **Act of consecration to the Sacred Heart of Jesus and the Immaculate Heart of Mary.**

"Lord Jesus, Chief Shepherd of the flock, I consecrate myself to Your most Sacred Heart. From Your pierced Heart the Church was born, the Church You have called me, as a member of Shepherds of Christ Associates, to serve in a most special way. You reveal Your Heart as a symbol of Your love in all its aspects, including Your most special love for me, whom You have chosen as Your companion in this most important work. Help me to always love You in return. Help me to give myself entirely to You. Help me always to pour out my life in love of God and neighbor! Heart of Jesus, I place my trust in You!

"Dear Blessed Virgin Mary, I consecrate myself to your maternal and Immaculate Heart, this Heart which is symbol of your life of love. You are the Mother of my Savior. You are also my Mother. You love me with a most special love as a member of Shepherds of Christ Associates, a movement created by your Son as a powerful instrument for the renewal of the Church and the world. In a return of love, I give myself entirely to your motherly love and protection. You followed Jesus perfectly. You are His first and perfect disciple. Teach me to imitate you in the putting on of Christ. Be my motherly intercessor so that, through your Immaculate Heart, I may be guided to an ever closer union with the pierced Heart of Jesus, Chief Shepherd of the flock."

17. **Daily Prayers.** All members should say the Holy Spirit prayer daily and make the act of consecration daily. They should also pray the rosary each day. They are encouraged to use the other above prayers as time allows.

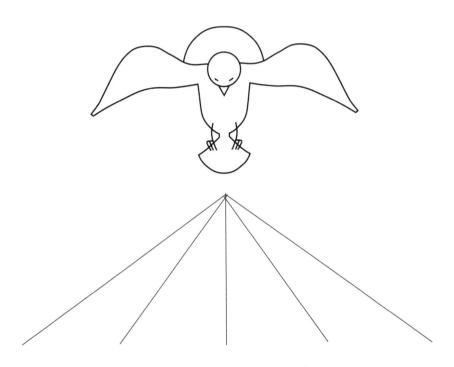

HOLY SPIRIT NOVENA

**The Holy Spirit Novnea prayers are
also available in
Spanish, French, and Portuguese.**

Shepherds of Christ Publications
China, Indiana

This book is published by Shepherds of Christ Publications, a subsidiary of Shepherds of Christ Ministries, a tax exempt religious public charitable association organized to foster devotion to the Two Hearts, the Sacred Heart of Jesus and the Immaculate Heart of Mary.

For additional copies, contact us:

Shepherds of Christ Ministries
P.O. Box 627
China, Indiana 47250 USA

(toll free number) 1-888-211-3041
(phone) 1-812-273-8405
(fax) 1-812-273-3182
http://www.SofC.org

Nihil Obstat:
Rev. Daniel J. Mahan, S.T.L.
Censor Librorum
Archdiocese of Indianapolis

Imprimatur:
Archbishop Daniel M. Buechlein, O.S.B.
Archbishop of Indianapolis
Archdiocese of Indianapolis

First Printing: March, 1999
Second Printing: April, 2000

DAILY NOVENA PRAYERS

Opening Prayer

In the name of the Father and of the Son and of the Holy Spirit. Amen.

Dear Father, we come to You in the name of Jesus, in union with Him in the Holy Sacrifice of the Mass, in the Holy Spirit. We come to You united to the Child Jesus of Good Health and the Infant of Prague. We come to You in the perfect, sinless heart of Our Mother Mary, asking her powerful intercession, uniting ourselves to her holy tears. We come to You united to all the angels and saints, and the souls in purgatory.

Prayer for Holy Spirit

We pray for an outpouring of the Holy Spirit on us, to be baptized by the Holy Spirit, that He will descend mightily on us as He did on the Apostles at Pentecost. That the Holy Spirit will transform us from fear to fearlessness and that He will give us courage to do all the Father is asking of us to help bring about the Reign of the Sacred Heart and the triumph of Mary's Immaculate Heart. We pray for the Holy Spirit to descend mightily on the Jesuits and the Poor Clares on the Shepherds of Christ leaders and members and on the whole Body of Christ and the world.

Protection by the Blood of Jesus

We pray that the Blood of Jesus will be spread on us, everyone in our families, and the Shepherds of Christ Movement, that we will be able to move steadfastly ahead and be protected from the evil one.

Healing

We pray for healing in body, mind, and soul and generational healing in ourselves, in all members in our families, and in all members of the Shepherds of Christ Movement, the Jesuit Community, the Poor Clares, the Body of Christ, and the world.

Prayer for Strength and Light

We adore You, oh Holy Spirit. Give us strength, give us light, console us. We give ourselves entirely to You. Oh Spirit of light and grace, we want to only do the will of the Father. Enlighten us that we may live always in the Father's will.

Eternal Spirit fill us with Your Divine Wisdom that we may comprehend more fully insight into Your Divine Mysteries.

Give us lights, Oh Holy Spirit that we may know God. Work within the heart, the spiritual womb of the Virgin Mary, to form us more and more into the image of Jesus.

Prayer to Be One with God, Father, Son and Holy Spirit

We long for You, Oh Spirit of Light, we long to know God, we want to be one with Him, our Divine God. We want to be one with the Father, know Him as a Person most intimately. We want to know the beloved One, the Sacred Heart of Jesus, and live and dwell in Him at all times, every moment of our lives. We want to be one with You, Oh Spirit of Light, that You move in us in our every breath.

Prayer to Be One in Jesus

Let us experience life in the Sacred Heart of Jesus, so we can say as Saint Paul, "I have been crucified with Christ and yet I am alive; yet it is no longer I, but Christ living in me...." Let us live, united to the Mass, all through the day being one in Him. Let us be able to love and know in this elevated state of oneness with our God. We long for Thee, oh beauteous God, we love You, we love You, we love You. We praise You, worship You, honor You, adore You, and thank You, our beloved God, Father, Son, and Holy Spirit.

Prayer to Dwell in the Hearts of Jesus and Mary

We seek to be one in God, to live and dwell in the Hearts of Jesus and Mary, our little heaven on earth, to experience life in the all perfect, pure, sinless heart of our Mother. We want the Holy Spirit to move in us and to be united to Jesus as the Bridegroom of our souls and be a most perfect sacrifice offered to the Father at every moment as we unite in the Holy Sacrifice of the Mass around the world to help in the salvation of souls.

Prayer for the Holy Spirit and His Gifts

Come Holy Spirit, come, come into our hearts, inflame all people with the fire of Your love.

Leader: Send forth Your Spirit and all will be reborn.

All: And You will renew the face of the earth.

We pray for the seven gifts of the Holy Spirit, we ask for perfection in our souls to make us holy, holy souls likened to God.

Dear Holy Spirit, we give ourselves to You soul and body. We ask You to give us the Spirit of Wisdom, Understanding, Counsel, Fortitude, Knowledge, Piety, and Fear of the Lord.

Prayer for the Word Alive in Our Hearts

We know, dear Holy Spirit, the Word in His human nature was brought forth within the womb of the woman. We pray that His word will be brought forth in our hearts as He lives and dwells in us. We want the incarnation to go on in our lives. Dear Holy Spirit, work in us.

Little Prayers to the Holy Spirit

Dear Holy Spirit, help us not to be ignorant or indifferent or weak, help us to be strong with the love of God.

Dear Holy Spirit, please pray for our needs for us.

Dear Holy Spirit, help us to respect God and to avoid sin. Help us to live in the Father's will.

Dear Holy Spirit, help us to keep Your commandments and to respect authority. Help us to love all things as You will us to love them. Help us to want to pray and always serve God with the greatest love. Help us to know the truth. Help us to have the gift of faith, hope, and love. Help us to know what is right and what is wrong.

A Prayer for Intimacy with the Lamb, the Bridegroom of the Soul

Oh Lamb of God, Who take away the sins of the world, come and act on my soul most intimately. I surrender myself, as I ask for the grace to let go, to just be as I exist in You and You act most intimately on my soul. You are the Initiator. I am the soul waiting Your favors as You act in me. I love You. I adore You. I worship You. Come and possess my soul with Your Divine Grace, as I experience You most intimately.

FIRST WEEK
MEDITATIONS NINE DAYS

1. Romans 8:14-17

All who are guided by the Spirit of God are sons of God; for what you received was not the spirit of slavery to bring you back into fear; you received the Spirit of adoption, enabling us to cry out, 'Abba, Father!' The Spirit himself joins with our spirit to bear witness that we are children of God. And if we are children, then we are heirs, heirs of God and joint-heirs with Christ, provided that we share his suffering, so as to share his glory.

2. Romans 8:5-9

Those who are living by their natural inclinations have their minds on the things human nature desires; those who live in the Spirit have their minds on spiritual things. And human nature has nothing to look forward to but death, while the Spirit looks forward to life and peace, because the outlook of disordered human nature is opposed to God, since it does not submit to God's Law, and indeed it cannot, and those who live by their natural inclinations can never be pleasing to God. You, however, live not by your natural inclinations, but by the Spirit, since the Spirit of God has made a home in you. Indeed, anyone who does not have the Spirit of Christ does not belong to him.

3. 1 John 4:12-16

No one has ever seen God, but as long as we love one another God remains in us and his love comes to its perfection in us. This is the proof that we remain in him and he in us, that he has given us a share in his Spirit. We ourselves have seen and testify that the Father sent his Son as Saviour of the world. Anyone who acknowledges that Jesus is the Son of God, God remains in him and he in God. We have recognised for ourselves, and put our faith in, the love God has for us. God is love, and whoever remains in love remains in God and God in him.

4. 1 John 4:17-21

Love comes to its perfection in us when we can face the Day of Judgement fearlessly, because even in this world we have become as he is. In love there is no room for fear, but perfect love drives out fear, because fear implies punishment and no one who is afraid has come to perfection in love. Let us love, then, because he first loved us. Anyone who says 'I love God' and hates his brother, is a liar, since whoever does not love the brother whom he can see cannot love God whom he has not seen. Indeed this is the commandment we have received from him, that whoever loves God, must also love his brother.

5. 1 John 4:7-11

My dear friends, let us love one another, since love is from God and everyone who loves is a child of God and knows God. Whoever fails to love does not know God, because God is love. This is the revelation of God's love for us, that God sent his only Son into the world that we might have life through him. Love consists in this: it is not we who loved God, but God loved us and sent his Son to expiate our sins. My dear friends, if God loved us so much, we too should love one another.

6. Acts of the Apostles 1:1-5

In my earlier work, Theophilus, I dealt with everything Jesus had done and taught from the beginning until the day he gave his instructions to the apostles he had chosen through the Holy Spirit, and was taken up to heaven. He had shown himself alive to them after his Passion by many demonstrations: for forty days he had continued to appear to them and tell them about the kingdom of God. While at table with them, he had told them not to leave Jerusalem, but to wait there for what the Father had promised. 'It is', he had said, 'what you have heard me speak about: John baptised with water but, not many days from now, you are going to be baptised with the Holy Spirit.'

7. Acts of the Apostles 1:6-9

Now having met together, they asked him, 'Lord, has the time come for you to restore the kingdom to Israel?' He replied, 'It is not for you to know times or dates that the Father has decided by his own authority, but you will receive the power of the Holy Spirit which will come on you, and then you will be my witnesses not only in Jerusalem but throughout Judaea and Samaria, and indeed to earth's remotest end.'

As he said this he was lifted up while they looked on, and a cloud took him from their sight.

8. Acts of the Apostles 1:12-14

So from the Mount of Olives, as it is called, they went back to Jerusalem, a short distance away, no more than a Sabbath walk; and when they reached the city they went to the upper room where they were staying; there were Peter and John, James and Andrew, Philip and Thomas, Bartholomew and Matthew, James son of Alphaeus and Simon the Zealot, and Jude son of James. With one heart all these joined constantly in prayer, together with some women, including Mary the mother of Jesus, and with his brothers.

9. Acts of the Apostles 2:1-4

When Pentecost day came round, they had all met together, when suddenly there came from heaven a sound as of a violent wind which filled the entire house in which they were sitting; and there appeared to them tongues as of fire; these separated and came to rest on the head of each of them. They were all filled with the Holy Spirit and began to speak different languages as the Spirit gave them power to express themselves.

SECOND WEEK
MEDITATIONS NINE DAYS

1. **John 14:21-31**
   Whoever holds to my commandments and keeps them is the one who loves me; and whoever loves me will be loved by my Father, and I shall love him and reveal myself to him.'

   Judas—not Judas Iscariot—said to him, 'Lord, what has happened, that you intend to show yourself to us and not to the world?' Jesus replied:

   'Anyone who loves me will keep my word, and my Father will love him, and we shall come to him and make a home in him. Anyone who does not love me does not keep my words. And the word that you hear is not my own: it is the word of the Father who sent me. I have said these things to you while still with you; but the Paraclete, the Holy Spirit, whom the Father will send in my name, will teach you everything and remind you of all I have said to you. Peace I bequeath to you, my own peace I give you, a peace which the world cannot give, this is my gift to you. Do not let your hearts be troubled or afraid. You heard me say: I am going away and shall return. If you loved me you would be glad that I am going to the Father, for the Father is greater than I. I have told you this now, before it happens, so that when it does happen you may believe.

   'I shall not talk to you much longer, because the prince of this world is on his way. He has no power over me, but the world must recognise that I love the Father and that I act just as the Father commanded. Come now, let us go.

2. **John 17:11-26**
   I am no longer in the world, but they are in the world, and I am coming to you. Holy Father, keep those you have given me true to your name, so that

they may be one like us. While I was with them, I kept those you had given me true to your name. I have watched over them and not one is lost except one who was destined to be lost, and this was to fulfil the scriptures. But now I am coming to you and I say these things in the world to share my joy with them to the full. I passed your word on to them, and the world hated them, because they belong to the world no more than I belong to the world. I am not asking you to remove them from the world, but to protect them from the Evil One. They do not belong to the world any more than I belong to the world. Consecrate them in the truth; your word is truth. As you sent me into the world, I have sent them into the world, and for their sake I consecrate myself so that they too may be consecrated in truth. I pray not only for these but also for those who through their teaching will come to believe in me. May they all be one, just as, Father, you are in me and I am in you, so that they also may be in us, so that the world may believe it was you who sent me. I have given them the glory you gave to me, that they may be one as we are one. With me in them and you in me, may they be so perfected in unity that the world will recognise that it was you who sent me and that you have loved them as you have loved me.

Father, I want those you have given me to be with me where I am, so that they may always see my glory which you have given me because you loved me before the foundation of the world. Father, Upright One, the world has not known you, but I have known you, and these have known that you have sent me. I have made your name known to them and will continue to make it known, so that the love with which you loved me may be in them, and so that I may be in them.

3. 1 Corinthians 15:20-28

In fact, however, Christ has been raised from the dead, as the first-fruits of all who have fallen asleep. As it was by one man that death came, so through one man has come the resurrection of the dead. Just as all die in Adam, so in Christ all will be brought to life; but all of them in their proper order: Christ the first-fruits, and next, at his coming, those who belong to him. After that will come the end, when he will hand over the kingdom to God the Father, having abolished every principality, every ruling force and power. For he is to be king until he has made his enemies his footstool, and the last of the enemies to be done away with is death, for he has put all things under his feet. But when it is said everything is subjected, this obviously cannot include the One who subjected everything to him. When everything has been subjected to him, then the Son himself will be subjected to the One who has subjected everything to him, so that God may be all in all.

4. Revelation 3:1-3,12,16-19

'Write to the angel of the church in Sardis and say, "Here is the message of the one who holds the seven spirits of God and the seven stars: I know about your behaviour: how you are reputed to be alive and yet are dead. Wake up; put some resolve into what little vigour you have left: it is dying fast. So far I have failed to notice anything in your behaviour that my God could possibly call perfect; remember how you first heard the message. Hold on to that. Repent! If you do not wake up, I shall come to you like a thief, and you will have no idea at what hour I shall come upon you.

Anyone who proves victorious I will make into a pillar in the sanctuary of my God, and it will stay there for ever; I will inscribe on it the name of my God and the name of the city of my God, the new Jerusalem which is coming down from my God in heaven, and my own new name as well.

'...but since you are neither hot nor cold, but only lukewarm, I will spit you out of my mouth. You say to yourself: I am rich, I have made a fortune and have everything I want, never realising that you are wretchedly and pitiably poor, and blind and naked too. I warn you, buy from me the gold that has been tested in the fire to make you truly rich, and white robes to clothe you and hide your shameful nakedness, and ointment to put on your eyes to enable you to see. I reprove and train those whom I love: so repent in real earnest.'

5. Revelation 5:9-14

They sang a new hymn: You are worthy to take the scroll and to break its seals, because you were sacrificed, and with your blood you bought people for God of every race, language, people and nation and made them a line of kings and priests for God, to rule the world.

In my vision, I heard the sound of an immense number of angels gathered round the throne and the living creatures and the elders; there were ten thousand times ten thousand of them and thousands upon thousands, loudly chanting:

Worthy is the Lamb that was sacrificed to receive power, riches, wisdom, strength, honour, glory and blessing. Then I heard all the living things in creation—everything that lives in heaven, and on earth, and under the earth, and in the sea, crying:

To the One seated on the throne and to the Lamb, be all praise, honour, glory and power, for ever and ever.

And the four living creatures said, 'Amen'; and the elders prostrated themselves to worship.

6. Revelation 7:14-17

I answered him, 'You can tell me, sir.' Then he said, 'These are the people who have been through the great trial; they have washed their robes white again in the blood of the Lamb. That is why they are standing in front of God's throne and serving him day and night in his sanctuary; and the One who sits on the throne will spread his tent over them. They will never hunger or thirst again; sun and scorching wind will never plague them, because the Lamb who is at the heart of the throne will be their shepherd and will guide them to springs of living water; and God will wipe away all tears from their eyes.'

7. Revelation 12:1-8

Now a great sign appeared in heaven: a woman, robed with the sun, standing on the moon, and on her head a crown of twelve stars. She was pregnant, and in labour, crying aloud in the pangs of childbirth. Then a second sign appeared in the sky: there was a huge red dragon with seven heads and ten horns, and each of the seven heads crowned with a coronet. Its tail swept a third of the stars from the sky and hurled them to the ground, and the dragon stopped in front of the woman as she was at the point of giving birth, so that it could eat the child as soon as it was born. The woman was delivered of a boy, the son who was to rule all the nations with an iron sceptre, and the child was taken straight up to God and to his throne, while the woman escaped into the desert, where God had prepared a place for her to be looked after for twelve hundred and sixty days.

And now war broke out in heaven, when Michael with his angels attacked the dragon. The dragon fought back with his angels, but they were defeated and driven out of heaven.

8. Revelation 14:1-7

Next in my vision I saw Mount Zion, and standing on it the Lamb who had with him a hundred and forty-four thousand people, all with his name and his Father's name written on their foreheads. I heard a sound coming out of heaven like the sound of the ocean or the roar of thunder; it was like the sound of harpists playing their harps. There before the throne they were singing a new hymn in the presence of the four living creatures and the elders, a hymn that could be learnt only by the hundred and forty-four thousand who had been redeemed from the world. These are the sons who have kept their virginity and not been defiled with women; they follow the Lamb wherever he goes; they, out of all people, have been redeemed to be the first-fruits for God and for the Lamb. No lie was found in their mouths and no fault can be found in them.

Then I saw another angel, flying high overhead, sent to announce the gospel of eternity to all who live on the earth, every nation, race, language and tribe. He was calling, 'Fear God and glorify him, because the time has come for him to sit in judgement; worship the maker of heaven and earth and sea and the springs of water.'

Revelation 19: 7-8
let us be glad and joyful and give glory to God, because this is the time for the marriage of the Lamb. His bride is ready, and she has been able to dress herself in dazzling white linen, because her linen is made of the good deeds of the saints.'

9. Revelation 21:1-10
Then I saw a new heaven and a new earth; the first heaven and the first earth had disappeared now, and there was no longer any sea. I saw the holy city, the new Jerusalem, coming down out of heaven from God, prepared as a bride dressed for her husband. Then I heard a loud voice call from the throne, 'Look, here God lives among human beings. He will make his home among them; they will be his people, and he will be their God, God-with-them. He will wipe away all tears from their eyes; there will be no more death, and no more mourning or sadness or

pain. The world of the past has gone.'

Then the One sitting on the throne spoke. 'Look, I am making the whole of creation new. Write this, "What I am saying is trustworthy and will come true." ' Then he said to me, 'It has already happened. I am the Alpha and the Omega, the Beginning and the End. I will give water from the well of life free to anybody who is thirsty; anyone who proves victorious will inherit these things; and I will be his God and he will be my son. But the legacy for cowards, for those who break their word, or worship obscenities, for murderers and the sexually immoral, and for sorcerers, worshippers of false gods or any other sort of liars, is the second death in the burning lake of sulphur.'

One of the seven angels that had the seven bowls full of the seven final plagues came to speak to me and said, 'Come here and I will show you the bride that the Lamb has married.' In the spirit, he carried me to the top of a very high mountain, and showed me Jerusalem, the holy city, coming down out of heaven from God.

Revelation 22:20

The one who attests these things says: I am indeed coming soon.

Amen; come, Lord Jesus.

 Scriptural quotations are taken from
The New Jerusalem Bible, Doubleday & Co.
Imprimatur granted by Cardinal Hume.

Prayer for Union with Jesus

Come to me, Lord, and possess my soul. Come into my heart and permeate my soul. Help me to sit in silence with You and let You work in my heart.

I am Yours to possess. I am Yours to use. I want to be selfless and only exist in You. Help me to spoon out all that is me and be an empty vessel ready to be filled by You. Help me to die to myself and live only for You. Use me as You will. Let me never draw my attention back to myself. I only want to operate as You do, dwelling within me.

I am Yours, Lord. I want to have my life in You. I want to do the will of the Father. Give me the strength to put aside the world and let You operate my very being. Help me to act as You desire. Strengthen me against the distractions of the devil to take me from Your work.

When I worry, I have taken my focus off of You and placed it on myself. Help me not to give in to the promptings of others to change what in my heart You are making very clear to me. I worship You, I adore You and I love You. Come and dwell in me now.

150 Year Celebration of St Boniface as a Parish and Father Joe's 50th Celebration of Ordination

Rita Robinson Ring and Fr. Joseph Robinson

Other great books published by Shepherds of Christ Publications

(To order call or write us at address in front of book)

Shepherds of Christ Prayer Manual
The Shepherds of Christ has prayer chapters all over the world praying for the priests, the Church and the world. These prayers that Father Carter compiled in the summer of 1994 began this worldwide network of prayer. Currently the prayers are in eight languages with the Church's *Imprimatur*. We have prayed daily for the priests, the Church, and the world since 1994. Associates are called to join prayer Chapters and help us circulate the newsletter centered on spreading devotion to the Sacred Heart and Immaculate Heart and helping to renew the Church through greater holiness. Please form a Prayer Chapter & order a Prayer Manual. Item P1 - $0.50

Spirituality Handbook Fr. Edward Carter, S.J. did 3 synopsis of the spiritual life. *The Spirituality Handbook, the Priestly Newsletter 2000 Issue 3* and the *Tell My People* book. The way of spiritual life proposed to the members of Shepherds of Christ Associates is centered in consecration to the Hearts of Jesus and Mary. All aspects of the spiritual life discussed below should be viewed as means to help members develop their lives in consecration to Christ, the Sacred Heart, and to Mary, the Immaculate Heart. Item P2 - $3

Fr. Edward J. Carter S.J.

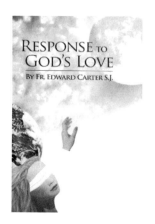

Response to God's Love by Fr. Edward J. Carter, S.J. In this book Fr. Carter speaks of God as the ultimate mystery. We can meditate on the interior life of the Trinity. Fr. Carter tells us about our uniqueness in the Father's Plan for us, how the individual Christian, the Church and the world are in the state of becoming. *Imprimatur*. Item BN4 -$10

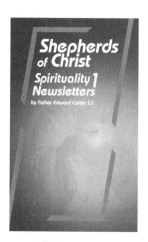

Shepherds of Christ - Selected Writings on Spirituality for all People as Published in Shepherds of Christ Newsletter for Priests. Contains 12 issues of the newsletter from July/August 1994 to May/June 1996. Item BN1 - $15

Shepherds of Christ - Volume 2 by Fr. Edward J. Carter, S.J. Contains issues 13-29 of the Priestly newsletter (September / October 1996 - Issue 5, 1999) Item BN2 - $15

Fr. Edward J. Carter S.J.

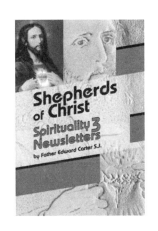

Shepherds of Christ - Volume 3 by Fr. Edward J. Carter, S.J. Contains Priestly Newsletter Issues 1 through 4 of 2000 including Fr. Carter's tremendous *Overview of the Spiritual Life*
Item BN3 - $10

Rita Ring

Mass Book, by Rita Ring. Many of the entries in the Priestly Newsletter Volume II from a spiritual journal came from this book. These entries are to help people to be more deeply united to God in the Mass. This book is available in English and Spanish with the Church's *Imprimatur*.
Item B8 - $12

Parents and Children's Rosary Book, by Rita Ring. Short Meditations for both parents and children to be used when praying the rosary. These medi-tations will help all to know the lives of Jesus and Mary alive in their Hearts. Available in both English and Spanish with the Church's *Imprimatur*.
Item B7 - $10

Fr. Joe Robinson
(Rita Ring's Brother)

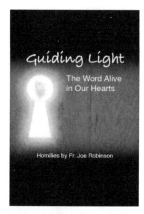

Guiding Light - The Word Alive in Our Hearts. - Cycle A (partial) — Homilies by the Reverend Joe Robinson given at St. Boniface Church in Cincinnati, Ohio. It is a tremendous honor Fr. Joe has allowed us to share these great gifts with you — for greater holiness and knowing more and more about God. Item C1 - $5

Guiding Light - Focusing on the Word - Cycle B — At times we may feel that our path to Christ is a bit "out of focus". Like the disciples in the Book of Mark, this ordinary life clouds our vision of Christ's Divinity. We may doubt the practicality or possibility of applying His teachings and example to our modern life. Cycle B's homilies are a "guiding light" to help us realize Jesus' Messianic greatness and His promise of better things to come. Item C2 - $15

Guiding Light - Feed My Soul - Cycle C — In a world rapidly advancing and encouraging personal gain, we are faced with modern problems. There is a challenge to find time in our busy schedules for Sunday Mass or a family meal. We are able to research, shop, bank and even work without hearing one human voice. It is no wonder that we may often feel disconnected and famished at our week's end. In Fr. Joe's third book of homilies from Cycle C, we are reminded of the charity that Christ intended us to show each other. .... We are rewarded with the Father's kingdom and love when we are not worthy. We are not left alone or hungry. Item C3 - $15

Guiding Light homily series - Steadfast to the Son - Cycle A — The sunflower is a great example of how we should be steadfastly guided by light. What a powerful thought that this exceptional plant is not stuck in one pose day in and day out, yet adaptable and magnetized to the sun. We feel the same about our Son. Our heads turns to face Christ as each day presents its challenges to find light. We join together like plants in a field and soak up the Son through the pulpit. We are a warm circle of strength using the wind of our breath to carry our priests' words, Christ's words, to new rich soil. Item C4 - $15

Guiding Light - Reflect on the Word - Cycle B — The Word leaves an impression on our souls. In my thoughts and reflections are born a more tangible understanding of these eternal concepts presented in the Gospels and the readings. Anyone can read a sentence, but not anyone can absorb it's true meaning. Truth, in this day and age, is almost a matter of opinion or individual entitlement. We believe that Christ's truth is our Roman Catholic Church. We, as priests, champion it's teachings; we are ambassadors for the Pope and Christ to those faces looking at us. We are the light by which our congregation reads to reflect upon real truth and we do it hand in hand. Item C5 - $15

Guiding Light - Centered In Christ, Cycle C — In the gospel of St. Luke, Christ turns toward Jerusalem, making the choice of love through sacrifice. In the silence of our own hearts, we find a worthy call to action. What personal path will you chose as you center in Jesus Christ? Fr. Joseph Robinson has dedicated his life to serving Christ and the Church from the Cincinnati Archdiocese in Ohio for over 40 years. He inspires his parishioners with the homilies found in these pages. ... May they be a guiding light for you as they have been for so many others. Item C6 -$10

Featured Selections

Response in Christ by Fr. Carter

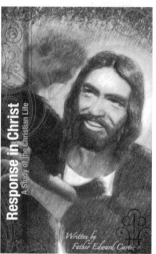

The book, **Response in Christ,** comes at a very opportune time. In a thoughtful blend of the traditional and the modern, Fr. Carter gives to the modern Christian a message that will sustain him.

The most promising aspect of the book is Fr. Carter's gift about the Spiritual life. The Christian life essentially consists in God's loving self-communication to us with our response to Him in love. God gives us a sharing in His life in baptism. This life is nourished by the Eucharist. Father Carter offers reflections on how to deepen one's relationship with God: Father, Son and Holy Spirit. Item BN5 -$10

Inspired To Be Genuine by Fr. Joe Robinson

Guiding Light - Inspired To Be Genuine, Cycle A Homilies

We look over the pulpit, like a father over Sunday breakfast and we want to connect. We want our parishioners to know the fulfillment, wisdom and desire that inspired our vows. We want them to find Christ and each other in Christ. Like a father, we want their attention, love and respect.

Privately, their minds may be elsewhere: in the next meeting, compiling a grocery list, worrying about a child, or angry with their spouse. We all leave a proverbial tornado of obligatory noise at the church doors to enjoy a single hour of unhurried glory.

... Father Joe Robinson inspires this appreciation into focus with humor, interesting facts and fresh perspectives. His homilies are easily followed, yet "meaty". May we all succeed to enliven a tangible God in the heart's forefront of those who hear us. Item C7 - $10

Shepherds of Christ Ministries

(You may copy this page to order.)

<u>Send Order To:</u>
Shepherds of Christ Ministries
P.O. Box 627
China, Indiana 47250 USA

Order Form

	<u>Qty</u>	<u>Total $</u>
P1. Prayer Manuals ($0.50)	___	___
P2. Spirituality Handbook ($3)	___	___
BN1. Shepherds of Christ - Volume 1 ($15)	___	___
BN2. Shepherds of Christ - Volume 2 ($15)	___	___
BN3. Shepherds of Christ - Volume 3 ($10)	___	___
BN4. Response to God's Love ($10)	___	___
BN5. Response in Christ ($10)	___	___
B7. Parents and Children's Rosary Book($10)	___	___
B8. Mass Book ($12)	___	___
C1. The Word Alive in Our Hearts ($5)	___	___
C2. Focusing on the Word - Cycle B ($15)	___	___
C3. Feed My Soul - Cycle C ($15)	___	___
C4. Steadfast to the Son - Cycle A ($15)	___	___
C5. Reflect on the Word - Cycle B ($15)	___	___
C6. Centered in Christ - Cycle C ($10)	___	___
C7. Inspired To Be Genuine - Cycle A ($10)	___	___
Totals:	___	___

Name: _____

Address: _____

City: _____ State: _____ Zip: _____

For More Information Call Toll free USA: 1-888-211-3041
or on the Internet: www.sofc.org

We pray for you from our Church in China,
24 hours a day before the exposed Eucharist.
We pray eight-day retreats for you every month.